Asperger's

A Literal Journey

DAVID MARR

Copyright © 2016 David Marr

All Rights Reserved. No part(s) of this book may be reproduced, distributed or transmitted in any form, or by any means, or stored in a database or retrieval systems without prior expressed written permission of the author of this book.

ISBN: 978-1-5356-0221-1

Contents

An Introduction by David's Big Sister vii
Prologue ix
Early Years 1
First Grade: Age Six 3
Second Grade: Age Seven 5
Third Grade: Age Eight 7
Karate 9
Pizza: Age Nine 11
Fourth Grade: Age Nine 15
Fifth Grade: Age Ten 17
Corinne St. Claire's Story 21
Kaiser Assessment 23
Sixth Grade: Age Eleven 27
Seventh Grade: Age Twelve 31
Eighth Grade: Age Thirteen 33
"Can you hold it?" 37
Ninth Grade: Age Fourteen 39
Ninth Grade: Second Semester 45
Aunt Suzy's Hint 51
Tenth Grade: Age Fifteen 53
Eleventh Grade: Age Sixteen 63
Pasadena City College 73
"Guy that hugs everybody" 83
Diagnosis at Twenty 85
Speech Class 87
Theater Arts Class 89
In-N-Out Burger 91
"Things sound nicer when you smile" 101
Driver's License 103
An Abusive Relationship 109

Massage School	113
Meeting Adam	115
Surprise Speech	119
Mom's Sickness	123
Struggling with Adam	127
Separation	131
YouTube	133
Walmart	137
Acting	149
Karaoke	153
Wallyball	157
"Good With Kids"	159
Coping with Asperger's	161
Surprise	165

My sister Erin and I.

An Introduction by David's Big Sister

In the fall of 2000, I was living in Pittsburgh, PA, and came back to Los Angeles to visit family. David had been unable to attend my wedding that July. He and Leslie (David's mom, my stepmom) had stayed in Los Angeles after David was hospitalized for depression. During my visit, David and I took a walk and had a long talk on the steps of the outdoor amphitheater at the nearby campus of Occidental College. It's a conversation that has stayed with me over the years because I felt both powerless to help and hopeful that things would get better for David. He had had such a long struggle in his earlier years with bullying and teachers who didn't get him. Now he seemed to be struggling mostly with our parents, frustrated with their restrictions and expectations. I remember telling him that I wished I could fast-forward him into adulthood when I envisioned him happier.

Fifteen years after that talk, I finally got to be with David at a July wedding — his own. He and Adam had met seven years earlier, during Leslie's illness. It was a complicated time. In May of that year, I was unable to travel to L.A. for a special Mother's Day/birthday celebration for Leslie. The family planned a short trip to Catalina Island — the site of family vacations when the boys were little. Adam flew out from Arkansas so that he could meet the family. I later heard from both Leslie and Grandma how much they liked him. They got to know him first over lunch at a favorite restaurant, and then as they toured the island in a golf cart that Adam rented for the occasion. Leslie lost much of her ability to communicate over the course of that year, but it was clear to me that she was happy that David had found someone so good and kind and supportive to build a life with.

As a sister, a daughter, and a parent, David's book is painful for me to read. It speaks to the things we get wrong when we don't understand someone we love, the hurt that can be caused when difficult issues aren't spoken of openly, and what may be gained by listening more closely to the quieter voices among us. David's book makes me consider my own choices as a parent even as I fear the effect my limitations will have on my children. But ultimately, this is not a book about fear or pain — this is a book about resilience and redemption. We can get stuck in the hurts we have endured and in the hurts we have caused. We can live with that dark cloud. Or we can find another path.

David is unfailingly honest about what he struggles with, about what he misunderstands and about who he is and what he needs. He helps me know how to connect with him, and that is a gift. In helping me know how to connect more with him, I have learned how to connect with countless other people in my life. My understanding of the fact that we all process things differently is deeper because I know David. My appreciation of persistence is greater because I watched as David got his Associate's degree, a massage therapy certification, and Bachelor's degree, all while overcoming obstacles that I could only imagine. My recognition of courage is more profound because I got to see David go from a little boy who would only whisper what he wanted into a parent's ear to a grown man who speaks more openly about his feelings than most people I know. He has done hard work to understand and accept himself and to help me do the same. He continues to be an inspiration to me.

Prologue

Before beginning I would like to clarify a couple of things. Just because I disagree with things about my family does not mean we did not have good times growing up also. I will state my feelings about things as they come up, but it does not mean things were all bad. Had I written a book about playing video games and watching TV with my family, it would have been a boring book. I did not want to write a book about that, so I didn't.

If I found a story to be interesting enough and on-topic enough with Asperger's, it was written for this book. I wanted to show a large scope of misunderstanding social cues over time, as well as the symptoms of Asperger's and how they progressed, changed, got worse, or improved over time for me. A couple of parts don't seem to fit in with that logic, but they were included because in the grand scope of the story, and the relationships, they needed to be there.

At age thirty I do feel I have grown out of my Asperger traits, but it took work to get here. I do feel it would have been less work had I had behavioral counseling, but what little counseling I had was limited. With martial arts help I could have developed confidence, which also would have helped me make eye contact. As it was I was an easy target, since I was someone who never knew how to make any eye contact.

If our Asperger kids are not in behavioral counseling and martial arts classes, I would expect them to be bullied countless times all throughout growing up. I know I was. Many accounts of bullying did not make it into the book. I did not want the entire book to be about bullying.

While talking, getting the feeling of being stuck, like I could not figure out a word to say, would be an issue as well. I would get better at blurting something out in time. That was hard for a while and another thing that makes bullies prey on Aspies. Silence is acceptance and bullying is never acceptable. People will pick on people just because they can, and silence allows them to.

The book seems dark to me at times, although it was never meant to be a dark book. Life was not all bad, but this book was designed to jump to the important parts and the life lessons.

There are a few examples in the book of teachers not understanding me and this causing frustrations for both me and the teacher. Please take something from that. It may benefit the student to let the teacher know that the student has Asperger's, and that they don't always learn things the same ways.

In any case, I hope it can help people. I wrote it as the book I would have wanted to read when I was young. It would have helped me learn and have something to relate to when I felt so alone and confused sometimes. I also wrote it for the confused moms who have talked to me, so puzzled, trying to figure out the complexities that are the nature of Asperger's.

I hope that if the book helps you, as I wrote it to do, you will tell someone about it.

Me, young.

Early Years

The first clear indication that I had some level of Autism, or at least that I was different in some way, came to me in preschool. I did not want to hang out with the other kids and wanted to hang out alone. A concerned teacher, of course, would call home and let the parents know so that this type of situation could be "fixed."

I look at that now, though, and see that clearly I needed some type of sensory break. It can be relaxing for us to hang out by ourselves. I have wanted it and craved it many times, every day of my life. I never felt that this was something wrong with me, and it can be relaxing being away from noise. It is relaxing being with my own thoughts, since I have so many of them, all the time. It can be relaxing just to let them play out in my head without distraction. No diagnosis was made, though, and no level of Autism was known yet.

The other two things that occurred at a young age that made it appear I developed differently took place when I was two years old. Somehow I was able to jump from phonics to reading. It's something my parents told me many times, and something they regretted not videotaping. Words are different to us, even at that age apparently. Later I would end up being a good speller, as well as the best reader of my whole class for many years.

Mom also has told me memories of things like me being in the car with relatives when I was little and being able to easily sing every note of songs. They thought it was amazing and unique.

David Marr

Mom wanted me to start playing a musical instrument since she was a pianist, but I did not end up sticking with one. People with Asperger's are supposed to have a higher likelihood of being able to sing. It makes sense that we process sound differently, as well as how we hear sound more accurately. It never did make sense to me that some people can't hit the right notes when singing, since I never had that issue.

First Grade
Age Six

There were not big social issues that I was aware of early in my life. I feel that I socialized better in some of my younger years than some of my later ones. When we are young we are expected to be silly or weird or goofy and it is accepted. Although I don't remember it, my teacher Mrs. Hankee told my Mom that at one point she hovered over me for a second to show me something with my schoolwork. I looked up at her with my upside-down face and said, "I love you Mrs. Hankee." She needed to share it with Mom. I couldn't tell you why I did that, but I guess it made sense at the time!

Mom would also have a different kind of conversation with her soon after that, though, since she had to let her know that I kept eating things off the floor. At school we had giant chocolate-chip cookies for fifty cents. I would find nearly a whole one on the dirty cement ground sometimes and would eat it. It never occurred to me to ask Mom or Dad for fifty cents. Why do that when there were clearly cookies available on the ground? I won't lie: I had this habit for years. It didn't go away with one conversation. It was a mental disconnect that I had. It just seemed like available food.

My parents were perplexed by other behaviors around the house as well. One day I had a total anxiety meltdown because I didn't know what I wanted to be when I grew up. My parents stayed with me and prayed with me for quite a while. It freaked me out at the time that I did not know. These things take time, but my young brain couldn't understand that. The fact that I didn't know right then made it seem like something was wrong.

We would have parties or gatherings on occasion and even though my guests were supposed to be my friends, I would always, every time, for years, end up hiding in my room. Mom would come up and tell me I should play with my friends. "They're fine," I would say. They appeared fine and what I did somehow did not appear rude to me. Knowing what things were like to other people was not just difficult to understand, but impossible. It was a total mental wall.

It would also perplex Mom or Dad that whenever I was alone with my homework for a few minutes and they would come in to help me I did not even have my name written on it. I had not done one thing. This did not make sense to them at all.

Second Grade
Age Seven

Seeing a difference between words in some situations can seem impossible. Sometimes I would just be stuck, as if my head would freeze, and not have the words at all. Sometimes I felt like I knew the words, but that they were the wrong ones and no alternative options seemed to be available.

One day a dorky tattletale, TJ, said smilingly and jokingly, "David spit at me!" He wasn't even mad or grossed out or anything. What he meant was that an accidental spittle had flown out of my mouth and hit him, just while I talked, not spit. Technically it was spit, wasn't it? So technically I had, hadn't I?

Mrs. Hamlett asked me, "Did you spit on him?"

"Yes."

"YOU DON'T EVER SPIT ON SOMEONE!"

I was horrified and hurt. What did I do? Mom spoke with Mrs. Hamlett and she told Mom that if I did not do it I "should have said no." Saying "no" did not make sense to me with this situation, since technically, spit had hit him.

Third Grade
Age Eight

Things started to make a little less sense in some ways, and people would start to talk in fancier ways that sometimes would confuse me. There was an instance in school where some people were in trouble and the teacher said, "You know who you are." She was referring to some people in the class. I got scared and wondered aloud, what if I didn't know it was me? The teacher explained that if I didn't know then it wasn't me. Weird word games my mind would play on me. It seemed frightening to me; what if I didn't know?

My anxiety attacks started getting worse around this time. I had a substitute teacher, Mrs. Kolidinsky, who asked us to bring sports stuff like balls to throw around. I forgot to bring mine, which she said wasn't a big deal; we could play with each other. I got scared, though, and I hid. She saw me out a window later and got mad at me for it. I was missing for quite a while. I got so frightened over forgetting to bring stuff that I couldn't face the situation; plus, socializing with others randomly wasn't always my strong suit, especially when it was forced in a class.

I wasn't always bad, though. A friend from the time told me later on that she was shyer than me and I was friendly to her and seemed cool to her and other classmates. Once when someone was mean to her I told him to punch my cast (I had a cast on a broken left arm). He did, and then left her alone. I also frequently said the joke, "What's for dinner? Refried dog poop!" which stayed funny to me. I stole that from The Simpsons.

Other things that were happening in life at the time showed my sensitivity as well. I once accidently sprayed our roses with the garden hose when trying to water the lawn. I cried and was devastated I had ruined the roses. Mom explained to me that they grew back. I was so relieved. To ruin a pretty rose on purpose just seemed unspeakable.

Karate

There are certain things that stick out as the "biggest mistakes" that were made when I was growing up, and my experience in karate is what I found to be the biggest. It was an unfortunate case of Mom overreacting and me not understanding situations because I was so literal. If there is one thing I could change about my past that would have changed everything, it is this.

What I did not know at age eight, but would figure out later on in life, is that people pick on shy people. In order to have the confidence to not be picked on, people need to be able to make eye contact. Eye contact requires confidence, which I did not have. Being in some kind of martial arts growing up would have changed everything. I got into it as an adult, and it did change me and mold me, as it made me much more confident.

When I went to karate, I loved it. I started with the basics class. I learned things like how to do a snap kick while we all stood in line and did it. Pretty soon after we started, my older brother Philip went to the advanced class. I thought that seemed like a good idea, so I joined him.

Advanced class was a little more aggressive. We actually did one-on-one fighting. Somehow, Mom got wind of this and immediately pulled me out. No explanation was given. I knew that when Mom got on her high horse there was no dealing with her. I felt I had no choice but to accept it. I would later regret not making a fuss and letting her know how bad her decision was. But I was eight and shy, and probably lacked the words.

What I did not understand at the time was that she was not even trying to kick me out permanently. She just thought I was too little. This was not explained to me, though, or I would have kept asking to do it. It was not even expensive either, just a cheap karate class taken at the park. It was about five dollars a month.

Pizza
Age Nine

Having a lack of words to properly communicate situations was something that went on for a long time. The biggest struggle for me at home was when I would be totally ignored for pizza night. I was the second of four boys (all born within 5 years and 3 months) and we all got to pick our pizza for Mom and Dad's Friday date night, for which we always got a babysitter. We always got two pizzas, which was more than enough. I would be asked what kind of pizza I wanted and I would always say "cheese," to which Dad would immediately respond, with a smile, "Oh, you can take the pepperonis off," and immediately point at another brother for their response.

My parents thought they had come up with a solution for dealing with my overly fussy-eater brother Stephen, who only ate a couple of things. Mom later on would grow to resent having to make some extra food item such as chicken nuggets so that he would eat. She quit doing it, but that was years down the road. Stevie always needed to be accommodated. He was number three of the four boys. Andy was the fourth and Philip was my older brother. Erin, my older sister, was the only member of my family, besides Mom, that I felt was truly compassionate, but she moved away when we were young. (Erin is 11 years and 2 months older then Philip. Dad had her in a previous marriage. I was told when I was young we do not call her a "half-sister" because that is rude, so I never called her that and I still don't.)

The pizza thing came up over and over again. It would never end. I did not know why they wouldn't listen to me. "I want cheese," "Oh, you can take the pepperonis off," over and over again. Stephen was a fussy eater so having a whole pepperoni pizza for him just made sense to my parents.

What Mom and Dad didn't understand was that every time they ignored me I was hurt and angry. Every time I got my pizza I would do what they said: I would take the pepperonis off and eat a pizza with giant holes in the cheese, giving myself a gross pizza. I longed for a plain cheese pizza but could never have one. I never explained to them what it did to me; I would simply say that I wanted cheese when the time came and wonder why I was being ignored.

Years later when I referred this to my parents, to having big holes in my pizza over and over again, they clearly were embarrassed. They didn't realize it was causing that kind of a problem and that I'd kept eating a gross pizza. At one point Mom even said, "Yeah, you should've made a... bigger deal about that." Mom was evasive like that. Instead of a "You should have said [fill in the blank]," which is what she would normally say, she instead said I should have made a bigger deal about it. Because I did say something — they just didn't want to hear it.

It's important that we listen carefully to our kids. They may not give us a lot of hints. They may not spell out exactly what something does or the consequence of something; they may not have the words to explain. I know I didn't have a clue what to say to get them to listen to me. When it was time to pick out the pizza there wasn't time to talk about it. I never felt that talking to them about it later would make any difference, and so I would not think to do that. Why would I? They would not listen to me whenever I told them in the moment.

Being a literal person can mean that saying something one way makes you think it will work, but it can also mean you don't know another way of saying the same thing. Sometimes you have to say why you want cheese and why the pepperoni doesn't work. Sometimes one way of saying it will not be enough of an explanation for somebody else to understand.

Fourth Grade
Age Nine

When I got to school for my fourth-grade year, I was put in the gifted class. I felt good and proud of that at first, but I was in the joint fourth- and fifth-grade class. There were hardly any fourth-graders. This presented problems quickly. Jokes that seemed goofy and funny to make when I was in third grade no longer seemed funny to anyone. I learned not to make them.

There were good times and bad, though. I remember at one point socializing and having a lot of fun with group activities like kickball. I was having a fantastic day and after school was over Mom took me to some lady in an office. Mom started to go on and on about how I didn't have any friends. I was hurt over and over by the things she said and started crying. She didn't even ask me how I felt. She simply told the other lady how I felt. This seemed so strange and hurtful to me because I thought I was doing great that day. I was having a great time just being who I was, but maybe not having friends to hang out with on the weekend automatically made me a loner with no friends to Mom. She saw no point in asking how I felt about it; she just made assumptions.

Later I took my giant misstep that changed everything that year. I developed a crush on a twelve-year-old boy, Luis, when I was nine. I looked up to him and he seemed so handsome. So I chased him, not seeing anything wrong with it at the time. Boys soon called me "Gaylord" and I had no idea what that meant. I didn't even know what the word "gay" was.

I was mistreated for the rest of the year, and my social awkwardness only made it worse. It got bad enough that Mom's friend, Iku, who was watching me after school with my brothers, saw me cry every day and saw what a wreck I was. She finally tore into Mom about it one day, telling her she needed to stop thinking so much about her piano lessons and start taking care of her kids. Soon I started homeschooling for a couple classes for a while, and Mom kept a better eye on me.

The year felt awful and I begged to switch schools. What I didn't realize at the time was that if I had just waited till the following year the jerks would be out of my classroom. I feel that if I had stayed, I would have been fine. I was hurting and I asked to leave, then I transferred into a school that turned out to be a lot worse.

Fifth Grade Age Ten

I'm not sure why it seemed like a good idea for me to go to a small Christian school that looked like prison, where all the students had known each other since kindergarten. This was a bad idea. None of the students seemed to like me or want to get along with me. People were cold and awful. It wasn't long before I started begging my parents to switch my school again, but Mom said she couldn't until that year was over.

The one good thing that came from that school was the discipline. I started to be able to get good grades and my memory with classes became better. It was my first year wearing a school uniform.

My coordination in sports was bad at the time. I was shocked one day when, without thinking, I raised my right leg and brought my arms together and was actually able to stop a ball. Over time I would get better at sports, some more than others, but that seemed to be the beginning of that.

My imagination was huge at the time. For some years growing up I thought that stuffed animals were real, and I would talk to them as if they could understand me. I don't remember what year I stopped doing that, but it took quite some time. This was not at school, though.

This type of imagination carried over to other things as well. I was an odd kid. My social awkwardness made it hard to talk to people and my imagination would likely only make me more of an outcast, yet that didn't seem to stop me. For example, I had these Trapper Keeper folders with amazing designs on them, like one with these colorful tires on it. I would stare at them in awe as I would imagine gliding through space, and I would be able to see them turning and jump off of one to the other. I was in my own little world and there was no one to see it but me.

My video game obsession had started and would last some years as well. One game I played had a tremendous impact on me even though I only bothered to play it for a weekend rental. It was ClayFighter for the Super Nintendo. I had these colored pencils that I would play with and I would make them fight and do battle and hit each other while I would fantasize about the game. My teacher, Mrs. Stone, told me not to do that once and took them away.

The next day I did it again and strangely she didn't stop me, so I did that off and on the rest of the year. I probably did it more times than I'd care to think about, as it was the only memory that my classmate Debbie had about me, that I used to play with my pencils. Debbie was a shy girl who hardly ever spoke in class. She later got married to my brother Stephen, years down the road.

Toward the end of the year I was at some meeting with a counselor and there was a big dry-erase board where we wrote down four different schools I could go to. The ones listed were Area H Alternative School, Eagle Rock Elementary, homeschooling, and Pacific Christian. I had visited Area H Alternative School with Mom once and I did like it, although a lady warned Mom when we visited not to bring me there, saying I wouldn't do well because kids were mean there.

In this list of four school options, I liked every option except for one: Pacific Christian. As soon as I visited that school, I didn't like it. It was small and it looked like a park. Being there bugged me for reasons I couldn't explain. I liked all the other options way better. It didn't help that I was leaving a small school and suddenly was going to another small school. Why? It seems clear now that I needed to be going to a public school where I could meet other eccentric people like myself, not be bored with the same people all the time.

One day I went to Pacific Christian and started trying on the school uniforms in the bathroom and going out to show Mom how they fit. Why was I trying on outfits at this school when I didn't even want to go here? I wondered. Suddenly my choices in schools were void and Mom was just going to choose for me. In her mind, I had switched schools twice and needed to find some place I could go for a while.

Corinne St. Claire's Story

I remember several things about David from fifth grade at Westminster Academy because I was a huge jerk to him. I, too, hadn't grown up with the kids in our class since kindergarten (I arrived in fourth grade), and since I was half-Asian, half-Caucasian, some of the kids decided to pick on me for it. When David arrived in fifth grade and was somehow weirder than all of us current weirdos, their mockery switched from me (and some others) to him. Unfortunately, as a stupid kid, I joined them. David was generally quiet, but always with a smile on his face (unless he was being picked on). He always seemed to be lost in his own world, and looking back, I kind of envy him for it. We could be in the middle of math drills, and there was David, smiling to himself about something.

One thing that always stood out to me about David was the way he handled himself physically. He had a couple of "tells" or "tics" that he couldn't stop. For example, if he got something wrong, he would quite literally do this face-palm motion with both hands while simultaneously smiling. At first it seemed dopey, but what kid isn't dopey? As the year went on, this became his go-to "Aw, I got it wrong!" reaction, and some kids would make fun of him for it.

Another tell he had was to clasp his hands together, fingers interlaced, and then move his arms around in a sort of circular motion. When I first saw it, I thought it was his way of helping himself think, kind of like how some kids look at the ceiling when trying to spell out a word. For a fifth grader, it was quite weird, but if he had done it around today's EDM ravers, he would have had moves to beat the best of them.

David was not a bad kid, and he definitely wasn't dumb, even though kids liked to say he was, and you could tell the teachers were struggling with him as well. Even though I would pick on him, I actually enjoyed hanging out with David, and Harriet (another "social outcast" of the class). We would play handball, four square, and other games together. These seemed to be happier times than when we were all together with our fellow classmates and the pecking order was reestablished. It is truly unfortunate what kids do when they think they are right.

Corinne had spoken with me once about an incident that, when she wrote this for me (fifteen years after she told me), she could no longer remember.

She told me how one time her picking on me had gotten bad and that Mrs. Stone had found out about it. When I asked how, she said, "Harriet ratted us out." Mrs. Stone had a talk with her and yelled at her and made her feel bad about it, and she cried for hours on her bed and took it hard.

There were a couple Westminster kids I have some bad memories about, but I had no bad memories I could think of about Corinne. But she says she was bad.

In a way it is nice that people were looking out for me behind my back, and I had no idea about any of it at the time.

Kaiser Assessment

I found this in my medical records for an analysis someone had done of me in the fifth grade when I went to my Kaiser hospital. I appreciate the adult perspective of what I was like at the time and found it important enough to include.

CC: KEITHA SCOTT, M.D., PEDIATRICS
DATE OF CONSULTATION: 01/17/96
TYPE OF CONSULTATION: Outpatient School Clinic Consultation

This ten-year-old boy, who has always had problems in school, is very shy, and has no friends, trouble fitting in, seems awkward and strange according to the mother. He is overly sensitive. He works hard at studies, but has no retention of what he studies. He is unable to comprehend directions. The children tease him a great deal. He has recently switched to a private Christian school, where things are even worse. He is here to be evaluated for a learning disability and perceptual problems.

According to the parents' report, he has difficulty comprehending the written and oral material, seems to have perceptual difficulties which include focusing or fixating obsessively on perceived wrongs, inability to discern important facts from a mass of material, inability to ascertain a plot line while reading, lack of physical coordination, and failure to recognize what behavior is socially acceptable.

He has been successfully treated in elementary school for stuttering. His early infancy and childhood behavior was characterized by poor sleeping, colickiness, excessive crying, difficult to warm up to situations and new people, insecure, unable to separate from mother.

HIS CURRENT BEHAVIOR: Short attention span maybe, depending on what he's doing, easily distracted, hears but doesn't listen, has major problems following multiple directions, has difficulty concentrating unless he's in a one-to-one structured situation, he is inconsistent and erratic in his performance. He needs a great deal of supervision, works quickly, makes silly mistakes, has difficulty organizing his work, and he is very slow and pokey, and doesn't finish up his work in time. He is very moody, he angers and worries easily. He is sad. He is basically unhappy. He is fearful. He has very, very low self-esteem. He bites his nails. He has problems with friends, shy, he is a loner.

He gets picked on or teased. David was tested on 12/05/95 here in our school clinic. His age was ten years and five months. His grade was five.
- Audiovisual screening was within normal limits.
- The Peabody Picture Vocabulary Test maturation age was 9 years and 8 months.

- His visual-motor integration test was quite dramatic at 14 years and 0 months.
- Draw a Person age 9 years and 3 months.
- The Jordan left-right reversal test was within normal limits and above average at 11 years and 6 months.
- The achievement testing on the Spadafore word recognition at the ninth grade level, significantly above expectations and is oral reading comprehension was at the third grade level.
- Silent comprehension and listening comprehension were also at the third grade level. He can certainly read, but he has problems with comprehending and paying attention.

His spelling and the Brigance, sixth grade level, math fourth grade level, sentence memory third grade level. He was often shy during the testing, and said, "I don't know the answer to this, I don't know what to do with it." He was very reluctant to try things out.

This child appears to have Attention Deficit Disorder without hyperactivity and his having some secondary psychological problems and self-esteem as a result. I have suggested a trial of Ritalin SR 20 mg one after breakfast, and the short-acting Ritalin tablets 5 mg one at 4:00 p.m., and to get follow-back from the mother.

This Ritalin got me in trouble at school. It made my behavior worse and I had to stop taking it.

Sixth Grade
Age Eleven

At Pacific Christian there were a little fewer than one hundred people in the whole school. It was nice being able to meet everyone, and for the most part everyone seemed pretty nice at first. No one knew each other before this year. Everyone else was totally fresh to each other.

There were jokes I made at the time. I remembered having a good time a lot of times. The one that stood out was once when the class was being loud and I said loudly, "Boys are sooo immature!!" and the class went silent. Was my joke that bad? I wondered. Much later I would find out from a student, David Rodriguez, that when I said that Mrs. Bowers gave me the funniest look he had ever seen.

I made friends with Taylor and Steven. Taylor turned out to be a liar and Steven was a redhead whom nobody liked because he was obnoxious and had bad social problems. His parents filed a suit against the school because "people were bugging him." At the time, though, I felt the three of us were friends.

I began to play a video game that seemed to greatly influence my imagination in real life. A student, Zack, had loaned me the game EarthBound for Super Nintendo, where a boy, Ness, had psychic powers and could do things like heal people and unleash weird, gnarly psychic attacks! I was mesmerized by this game and its weird fight sequences and I wanted these powers!

Taylor had some kind of compulsive lying problem and wanted me to believe I had psychic powers. This made me feel special at the time, and we would try things together where I would try reading his mind and he went along with it. I'm not sure why he did this, but he didn't cause problems with it; it was just something to do, I guess. Sometimes Steven went along with things, but sometimes he didn't.

Another classmate, John, told me how Taylor and Steven were talking trash about me to people while he was nearby, and told me "Don't be his friend" about Taylor. I told Taylor and Steven the next day that I knew about all this and that they were bad friends and I didn't want to hang out with them anymore. They denied doing it at first, but I knew John was not lying to me.

I started to be better friends with John as the year went on. He was fun to spend time with and do video game stuff with, as we liked some of the same ones. Zack and I got along and made jokes about stuff too since he was a goofball. I know I loaned video games to him a few times.

I felt pretty good for most of this year, but there were still things that puzzled Mom. For reasons unknown even to me, I would go behind this building and just hide there after school. Mom didn't like this and noticed it over and over when she picked me up. Many years later I would learn and understand that people with Asperger's need "sensory breaks," and this felt like what I needed: just to be in a darker place without sound for a while.

I still didn't understand certain social cues either. Mrs. Bowers called Mom to let her know that everyone else ate quickly, standing up, and then would play basketball, while I would hang out by myself. What was wrong with hanging out by myself? Does someone just invite themselves over to play basketball? What if I didn't want to play?

It was important to Mom that I read for enjoyment, which I refused to do over and over again. There was a lot of pressure on me to enjoy reading and it scared her that I didn't like it, according to her.

During this sixth-grade year we went to an eye doctor for a routine checkup. I had conjunctivitis. He moved my eyelid back to show her just how bad it was. He told her that kids that had it half as bad as I did came in just for that. I had not said a word. I was reading in school while my eyes burned somewhat, and that was one of the reasons I avoided reading outside of school. Mom had no clue and wished I had made a bigger deal about it.

The school year would end and summer would begin. We did as we always did and went to Port Townsend, Washington, for the summer. Bike rides and family time were encouraged with outdoor adventures, but TV time was not. Mom made a contest where if we read for a certain amount of hours we got prizes. I was the only one who did it out of me and my three brothers, and I read all summer long. My favorite books were the *Wizard of Oz* series, which I read for more than five-hour stretches of time, even seven hours on occasion. I quickly got over a hundred hours and no longer needed to read for my prizes and stopped. Star Fox 64 was my final prize.

Star Fox 64 had a review I read over and over until I had it memorized. I talked about it to anyone who would listen. I talked about the main game, what it was like, all the multiplayer battle modes and what each one was like; I went on and on and on. It was torture knowing this was coming out in July, right when we were leaving that summer. When we got back to LA I ran up to my room to claim my prize. It was one of the games I ended up playing the most. Several classmates had it as well.

Seventh Grade
Age Twelve

It was in seventh grade that I started to like girls. I had all of the emotional feelings for them: crushes, feeling weird and clumsy around them. Physically, they did not do it for me, and it took time for me to figure out what I wanted with that.

However, for this year I did like girls, and one of interest was Tiffany. Tiffany had a friend named Laureina, and they were both immature sixth graders. For whatever reason Laureina would lie to me about how Tiffany liked me, even though she didn't. I made excuses to follow her around, which I believed she liked, according to Laureina, but then might be told to go away by someone, even Tiffany and Laureina. It was all confusing. Why tell me these things if they were untrue?

My friend Casey gave me her number and I called her to ask what was going on. I thought it was a good idea to disguise my voice as a girl, but then her mom got all mad and yelled at me for a long time and demanded to know what was going on. I cried and was hurt, but stayed on the phone until I became a crying wreck. Tiffany finally was able to talk to me and told me she considered me a friend. Later, at school, Tiffany told me her mom was sorry.

I played with my new friend Cesar on the hills sometimes. One thing we did was throw mud at the other while they were climbing up the hill and sing, "It's raining mud, hallelujah it's raining mud!" and we had fun together. When we left the hill I would frequently leave my items at the top, which would often be stolen or taken to the lost and found. I lost a Calvin and Hobbes book once, which made me sad, and yet I still kept doing it. I was way too trusting of people.

Later in the year I had a drama class, which helped me in unexpected ways. I liked my teacher, so I paid close attention and took careful notes. We were doing a Christmas play at church and I was having a hard time being enthusiastic and Mom was having a difficult time getting me to do anything with emphasis. But with a combination of my drama teacher and Mom tutoring me, I mastered my Christmas play part as an innkeeper, where I told someone off and said, "Ha!" and strutted away. People thought it was hilarious. Once I got out of my monotone I ended up having a lot of fun.

Bullying was worse this year and my grades went down as a result. There were certain things I probably should have told my parents about, like when Nathaniel walked up to me and punched me in the stomach for no reason. It was easy to get depressed this year about other stuff that was happening. Sometimes with bullies there is a ringleader who bands people together. Joshua went to Pacific Christian for the first half of sixth grade, but left for unknown reasons and then returned in seventh grade. He was a mean, rude person who did awful stuff to people and had minions to do what he wanted. He vanished after seventh grade was over and the class was better and happier for it. Bullying would happen off and on over the years, and with my shyness and bad eye contact I would draw it to me and not be sure what to do about it. My parents did not know what to do either.

Eighth Grade
Age Thirteen

Once I entered eighth grade I had a much more fun year. The bad kids were better, and since Joshua had left, the atmosphere was all-around better. I started to enjoy myself in talking more, and there were even girls that openly said they liked me, and that I was funny, while other girls agreed. I felt like I had it more together this year, and I had a good time in a lot of ways.

One struggle I had, though, was with my history class. I struggled for hours and hours with my parents while barely managing to get a D each semester. The teacher, Mrs. Underwood, was awful. One day when I knew I hadn't done well on a test I asked if she could put it face down and she said, "You should put YOUR face down for what you got on THIS test!!" She made excuses to Mom later about that, saying she felt it was okay to do that because I was joking about it. These kinds of things would keep happening and it would get worse.

My security blanket from sixth grade until the end of my Pacific Christian time was my sweater that I always wore with the PC logo on it. My thing, I told myself, was that it covered me well in case I got an erection. Did I ever get an erection during lunch or break, though? No, but it was what I told myself and the fabric was comfortable, so I always wore it, even on hot days. One day Mrs. Underwood took it away from me for no reason, but Mom made sure to get it back after class. Mom later regretted not taking more action against her, and was not happy about my experiences with her at all.

    I started talking on the phone a lot more, hours a day even, and my grades went up since I was happier, except for history, which I continued to struggle with. Although my socializing and happiness was a lot better, I still needed better friends and wasn't sure how to obtain them. My friend Jeremiah became my closest friend even though he was a compulsive liar, and over time I became closer to Joey, though he was a compulsive liar as well. He would also punch my arm, as a joke, over and over again. I never said or did anything about it because I thought that if I did it made me weak, but I didn't like it. John was around us too, and I should have made better friends with him but didn't. He wasn't a liar, and we drifted apart a bit. Cesar and I continued to be friends to a lesser extent until he was kicked out later that year for bad grades.

    Chris was a new student that year that I had a crush on, which I tried to hide. I just needed to be friends with him, and needed his approval, much more than anyone else's. He just seemed so funny with his jokes and his nice smile. He was a light-colored Mexican and was unintelligent but funny. We would hang out and talk on the phone.

    Without meaning to I called him too often, although to be fair there were times where he asked me to call him back and I guess he didn't mean it. One day he admitted he didn't want to talk to me. When I asked why not he said, "Because you're BUGGING ME!" I was scared and said my goodbyes. He started talking some trash about me, which I didn't think was fair. He did tell me to call him back, after all, and he handled his problems like garbage. Wasn't there a nicer way to tell someone to call less? He was not smart and he did not know a better way. It hurt me that other people liked him while I was having these personal problems with him, and yet he seemed unavoidable because everyone else hung around him.

Cesar and Chris both got notes on the same day asking them to go to the principal's office. They both were removed from school for their bad grades. Cesar and I kept in touch and hung out a few times after that. Chris returned for ninth grade and continued to be lazy and get bad grades and would be kicked out the next year too. Why bother returning to a private school if you aren't even going to try? But that's how he was.

There was one thing about Chris that I was grateful for, though. There was a time when I had a tune stuck in my head. I heard it from a cartoon on Nickelodeon called "KaBlam!". They all had the same tune stuck in their head and sang the same few notes over and over. I had it stuck in my head in a severe and bad way, off and on, but mostly on, for months.

I was scared it would ruin my life. I once told Chris about it and he asked to hear a couple of the notes, and when I hummed them for him he told me to sing the Budweiser tune because it was so similar. I did as he suggested, and poof! It was gone. The other stuff Chris did was awful, but I will always be grateful for that. OCD compulsions with Asperger's can take a life of their own, and I'm glad that tune didn't go farther than it did.

My closest friend for most of the year was Jeremiah. He lied about everything and would later say that he was joking and insisted that meant he wasn't lying. Joey did the same thing. From being around that, I started lying too, although I was not good at it, and it was a phase that went away when I was no longer around liars. Jeremiah also taught me how to be lazy and cheat my way through school all the time. At some point I finally got sick of doing this and got my act together. I was sick of feeling like a loser.

David Marr

My parents continued to confuse me a lot, and often made less sense than the other kids. One day my Dad asked if we could do some chores, acting as if it were a choice. When I declined, my brothers all went out and got video games from FuncoLand (that was what GameStop used to be called) and toys from other places, and they all showed off to me what great stuff they had. It seemed like my Dad asked them to rub my face in it, but why do this? Wasn't it a choice? Why were some things choices while some things were not? It made no sense.

"Can you hold it?"

One of the most unpleasant car experiences on our two-day road trips from Port Townsend, Washington, to Los Angeles, California, was when we were returning home to LA and I said I needed to go to the bathroom and was asked, "Can you hold it?"

What a complex question for someone with Asperger's. Well, can I hold it? I certainly can, I guess, but it does not mean it's pleasant.

It's unclear what made me need to pee so hard so fast. I didn't feel like I had drank anything. Suddenly, the pressure was so much I feared peeing in my pants. It never occurred to me to speak up. Can I hold it? I felt like I could.

The awful feeling like I was going to pee my pants any second just got worse and worse. Luckily I never did, but the feeling was constant and it lasted a long time. Finally, the car stopped at home and I raced out and climbed something to jump over our fence. I ran to go pee in the yard in the dark somewhere. My pee went out several feet in a monster rocket of pee. It was wonderfully relieving but horrible to experience beforehand.

Somehow this came up in reference with a story and my parents had no idea it was that bad and felt like I should have told them. But was it necessary? I already said I needed to go. It would have been nice to be listened to the first time. Sometimes we may lack the words for how technically we can hold it, but it can still be a terrible experience.

Ninth Grade
Age Fourteen

When my year of ninth grade started I had lost my friend, Joey, who didn't want to be friends with me anymore, and I was depressed. He'd told me he wouldn't care if I was gay when we talked about it, so I told him I was. We could no longer stay friends. He was an awful friend anyway, although I did not see it at the time.

My depression mounted, and my GPA slipped to beneath a 2.0. Suddenly I was in the room that people went to when their grades were bad for an hour after school. Being around Joey was difficult and he made sure to make rude comments to me and about me, which hurt. I was forced to try to socialize with new people.

One day I came to school and Zack told me there were more than five different people that told him that David had called them last night. I was calling new people, trying to socialize and have fun in the ways that I could, and this was because I could no longer hang out with my old friends due to Joey being there.

Mom and Dad had allowed an unheard-of luxury for me the summer before and allowed me to watch the horror movies I wanted to watch. I watched lots of different ones and enjoyed them, although binge-watching them after not being allowed to see them for so long may have helped create a bad effect.

I was on the phone with Chris and Zack one night, casually talking about usual teenager stuff on a three-way call. In front of me was this basket-shelf thing with Mom's piano stuff on it, and a big window next to me. I saw a hooded death figure run up to my brother's room outside. I freaked out and started telling my friends. They told me to hang up and call the cops. I looked back and the figure had an axe that was swinging towards the door. I went to the kitchen.

It turned out to be my brother's girlfriend, who was at the door. This experience freaked me out enough that I wrote about it. When Jeremiah read it, he insisted that the story keep going. It evolved to where different people had different visitors of creepy variations come to kill them at their house. Some of them even had superpowers, like the one based on our classmate, Leah, who could freeze time.

I didn't want to write the story at first; I only did it because Jeremiah insisted on it. With his imagination, and him acting like a kid, he wanted to insist that we would make a book and he would illustrate it and get half profits since he was poor. We would also make a movie about it, which he had "connections" for. I wasn't gullible enough to believe Jeremiah and knew he had some kind of lying disorder. It was fun making a story with him though, and I continued it. I had real first names of classmates, since it was easier to write it and visualize it that way.

One day I had about twenty pages of it written, but I could not give it to Jeremiah, since Jeremiah and Theo were trying to help Chris and Natalie learn how to make out. I was curious, but Jeremiah said they wanted their privacy. I hung out on the grass not too far away and heard a little bit of conversation before Jeremiah came up to me and basically asked me what I was doing and told me to go away. Giving the story to Jeremiah was not an option so I gave it to Jeremiah's grandma when I saw her, and she cheerfully agreed to pass it on. I thought nothing of it.

The grandma never caused any problems as far as I ever knew. She admitted to Mom once when I wanted to hang out with him that Jeremiah's mom was an overprotective wacko. It was known that I had given it to the grandma, though. I heard later on that Jeremiah's mom found it in his laundry.

Somehow, Jeremiah's mom read it and Jeremiah called me so she could talk to me. She talked to me for a long time and the conversation was all over the place. I did not have much room to talk at all. She talked to me about how girls liked tall guys, and different things about the story that disturbed her. There was a part where the character based on me, named David, had a dream where he killed someone with a knife and a wide smile appeared on his face. This part disturbed her. She acted as if she were my friend and told me that I could call her anytime, day or night. She told me enthusiastically that even if it was two a.m. I could call her.

What she didn't tell me was that she had gone to the principal with trembling hands with her copy of the story and told him if he didn't get me kicked out of school, she would have him fired.

I started class the next day and after my first-period class, Spanish, my parents were waiting for me. They asked me to get all my things and go to the car, so I did. They asked me if I'd gotten my flute from my locker. I had not, and also did not understand why this was necessary. They told me to get my things from my locker and go to the car.

I did as I was instructed, and my parents filled me in on all they knew about Jeremiah's mom. The next few weeks were a blur of trying to prove I wasn't crazy at Kaiser, only to find out that not only was I not crazy but I was "a genius." My ego was thrilled and my parents weren't surprised. There were meetings with detectives, and cops that went to the school to interrogate students. The cops were called there by our principal Dr. Riesen.

Leah and Joey were two classmates that had bad lying problems and made up the weirdest stuff about me. Leah said I wrote threatening letters, Joey said I left weird prank calls of villains from horror films like Chucky, Leah shared that one note said "DIE" with a knife stuck into it in her yard. Leah had some terrible mental problems and everyone knew she was a liar. One day my friend Carol demanded proof:

"Where are the letters, Leah?!"

"Oh, Dr. Riesen has them," Leah answered.

Ultimately, Mom, Dad, and I decided that even if we could go back to Pacific Christian we all didn't want me to. Dad was convinced that if I did, the principal, Dr. Riesen, would find some way to kick me out. They had different meetings with Dr. Riesen and in one of them he was trying to convince them that I was crazy. They said that they didn't trust him; they trusted their son.

"Well, what are we doing sitting here then?" Dr. Riesen replied.

"Exactly," both my parents said.

I went to an independent study after three weeks of being in no school at all, and was able to finish a few classes, including an English class and a calligraphy class. I got As in all of them, but somehow got a B in calligraphy.

Mom took my being kicked out of school extremely hard. I felt fine about it, although I wished I could have talked to my friends. But I could not do that because the police were involved, and the detective advised against it. One day my friend Brittany called to check on me and I gave the phone to my brother Philip, who explained the situation. It was the last call I got from any of them for some time.

Asperger's: A Literal Journey

While I was feeling good about leaving my school, apart from being unable to talk to any of my friends, Mom took things out on me and I was unhappy because of it. She demanded that I read books and do chores, and made more demands over and over again. One day she told me that when I did my schoolwork I could "party," so I did, only to find out that the only way I could "party" was to read books. Then she tried to clean it up by saying maybe her way of "partying" and mine were different. It was weird, and her constant resistance to my being able to watch TV became unbearable.

One day she acted like my health class work was due on one day when it wasn't, and I knew it was due the following day, so I didn't do any of it. She later admitted that she'd lied, but she just wanted me to do it. She got frustrated and told everyone that she wasn't going to help me with my schoolwork anymore, and I just thought to myself how glad that I was that she would leave me alone. Being the only person in the house with her was a nightmare, and she seemed to do all she could to take her aggression about the situation out on me.

One thing she liked to tell me was how hard it was on her that I was kicked out of school. She didn't seem to have any compassion for what was happening, but she argued that, as a parent, you'd always rather go through something yourself than see your kid go through it. If it was so hard on her, then why did she treat me so badly?

With the horror of Pacific Christian behind us, sometimes I would demand to know why I was forced to go there. Mom would get uncomfortable and smiley. She would say how I didn't like Eagle Rock Elementary, and didn't like Westminster, and I needed to go somewhere where I could stay for a while. I demanded more answers and she would start to walk away. I asked her to "let me finish!" and she would reply, "Oh you're never finished, you're never finished," and walk away with an obnoxious and uncomfortable smile on her face. The Pacific Christian situation was so hard on her that she refused to talk about it at all, even though I went there against my will and it was her idea, but she had nothing but resentment for that school after that. She even mailed my books there instead of just visiting the school to drop them off.

The teacher from my independent study knew Carol, an administrator from Eagle Rock High School, and although the school was capped and not allowing any more students, they were going to pull a favor and let me in. There was no time to look into other schools or pursue other options, at least none that we took the time to find out about. Abruptly, I was starting my first day of school in the second semester at Eagle Rock High School, my first time in four and a half years of being in a public school.

Some years later Pacific Christian no longer had the funding to continue operating as a private school, and it finished the school year and closed down. Some of us have gotten back in touch and have had informal reunions.

Ninth Grade Second Semester

When I started in ninth grade I was so grateful to be back at school. I was thrilled to do the schoolwork, and it was easy to want to get good grades. The classes were easier than what I was used to at my former private schools, and my grades were considerably better than when I was at Pacific Christian and classes there had become too difficult.

I was pretty quiet and shy but I got along with people. I took my brother Philip's advice, and just tried to be nice. "If someone needs a pen you give them a pen. Be nice to people and people will like you." On the other hand, though, he knew that bullying might become a problem and he told me to come to him if it did. That offer could only last till the end of my ninth-grade year, though, since he would be graduating. (Normally he would have been in 11th grade with our ages but years earlier had skipped a grade.)

I tried to make friends with a group of people that Philip introduced me to. I was shy, and it was hard. I would sit against a wall and they came up to me at first and tried to be nice. I hung out with them for a few weeks before I stopped.

There may have been some emotional overlap between the bad situation with Pacific Christian and Mom's later emotions. There was a report card I got where I was proud of my improvement with grades. The report card read A C A B A C. Mom got it, and she cried and gave me a guilt trip. She wondered why I got a B in Algebra 1A. She reminded me how she told me that if I got straight

As she'd get me a great present, but I couldn't even get an A in an easy math class.

It was such a surreal conversation, and I have no idea what was going through her mind or her emotions at the time. Here I was with these grades that a lot of parents would be happy about, and Mom cried and was upset about it. It was a push too much and I let my grades slide after that, since I no longer cared about trying to impress Mom. It's something I would regret not working out with Mom and Dad at the time, but I figured she would not regret saying what she said later anyway. It was the best report card I got at Eagle Rock High, and my grades after that would become considerably lower.

One day my friends Richard, Amber, Zach and I went to my back yard to smoke pot. It was a nice private area behind a fence with lots of dirt and just weeds. The land was part of our property, but it was too much land to look after so it just sat there in this weird hill shape. It wasn't flat. Richard told me that I should take five hits in a row and that I would get jacked up.

I did as he said, thinking nothing of it being a bad idea, and before I knew it I seemed to transform into another world. I spun around wildly, trying to pull hair out of my head. I heard a little girl's voice singing in the back of my head, "That's all right, that's all right, something in your conscience is trying to make sense" over and over again. Things felt like they rose for a few seconds and then just dropped over and over. I tried having a conversation with my friends and my memory and talking didn't seem to work right. At one point I asked Richard for his razor blade so I could cut myself open with it. Richard kept a razor blade on him to slice his arm a little bit from time to time.

Asperger's: A Literal Journey

My friends all left me there at my house. They didn't want to get in trouble, and my bad trip was only going to get them found out. The next day at school I walked up to them and, even though it was awkward, I made sure to make friends with all of them again, not holding anything against them. I didn't know who else to be friends with at school so it seemed like the thing to do.

Later for some reason I started talking to the school counselor and I let her know my experience. The thing with the razor blade got her attention and, although the counselor made it seem like I could trust her, I didn't expect it to lead to a hospitalization — and I didn't even know what that was.

Costa Mesa was a clinic which had some great counselors to talk to and I met other teenagers with problems. I got to see what other severely depressed teenagers were like. This experience made me want to be a counselor and to help troubled teens. Everyone just wanted us to be better. It was like a camp away from home and it felt good instead of bad. I regrettably had to miss my sister Erin's wedding because of being there, but aside from that there was definitely good that came from it.

Mom took the long drive out to visit me every day. She didn't go to the wedding either. At one point while I was there we had some kind of intelligence test with easy questions. There were three tests and on one I felt like I probably got one wrong. It turned out that I got 100% on all three.

It turned out Ian, one of the teenagers there, used to go to my school and was kicked out for dealing drugs. He spoke at the group meetings once about how he was impressed by my scores. He told me, "You got 100% on all those tests; you shouldn't be doing drugs." He talked about how much money he made dealing drugs but how it wasn't worth it.

It seemed that with Autism I was a scarily lightweight person when it came to substance abuse and people had to see it to believe it. Nobody thought I could get that high from so little and yet I could. I didn't stop smoking pot, but I smoked less at once. This sort of thing happened a lot, where I had bad friends and sort of made do, since being around bad company felt better than no company at all.

I finished the rest of the school year without too many problems, and summer came. We went to Port Townsend but I made a regrettable choice when I decided to write a letter to my brother Stephen's friend Jennifer, who was a family friend, and be honest about my sexuality, believing myself to be bisexual at the time. Mom said we needed to go and I left my letter on a table. I asked her not to read it. "Oh, don't worry, I have no interest in your letter," she said.

Later that day Dad drove me home and Mom confronted me in the driveway. She yelled at me about the letter, which she freely told me she'd read after telling me she would not read it. She made me go on a walk with her where she told me about a time where she saw how I looked at a girl that was trying to sell these massage packages. She didn't believe I could be gay. I found this strange since gay wasn't even the word I used in the letter. I said I was bisexual. The conversation ended with the walk and I went to bed later. Mom went to my bed and sat on it and cried and told me how it "just doesn't get any easier."

No more was said about any of this until months later when I had a private conversation with my Dad in my room. I was veering around topics a little bit, not exactly wanting to say that I was gay, or whatever I was. Dad surprised me by saying, in what he may have believed was a nice and considerate way, that "maybe homosexuality was something that I struggled with." "Struggle with" isn't the right phrase to use, though, and it is not nice or accepting at all, but my Dad did not know that.

If I could have had my way with this, my parents wouldn't have talked about the topic of sexuality anymore with me. I intended to keep that private and I knew they would only create problems about it. They were of an older generation, and they were Christians. There was never any part of me that believed they would be accepting of that. I tried foolishly to force them to accept it at times in conversations, which only became awkward, and so I stopped trying to talk about it.

Aunt Suzy's Hint

There were certain family members, like my Uncle Phil and Aunt Suzy, that we just saw in the summertime. They also had two kids, Aaron and Kaitlen. Kaitlen was around Philip's age and Aaron was a little older.

There were a few times where we had heard that Aaron had this amazing bachelor pad with tons of video games. Every time I heard about it, I was so pumped to see it.

One day we were invited to go to Aunt Suzy and Uncle Phil's house. It was the cleanest house I ever saw. I made a joke about how nice their house was and how ours could never be that clean. It was different to see such a clean house. I found out later that comment hurt Mom's feelings, which was not my intention. To me it was a given that in a house with a lot of kids, where we constantly had company over, things were just going to be messy. I now know moms are sensitive about that subject.

I thought it would be such a great idea to see cousin Aaron's amazing bachelor pad I had heard so much about, and so I asked about it. Aunt Suzy said that it was messy. I told her I did not mind that. Perhaps a normal person would have seen this as a hint, but I didn't. Why would I care if it was messy? I just wanted to play his video games.

At one point in this conversation I saw my older brother, Philip, saying "David" and when I looked over there, he mouthed the words "shut up."

What was he telling me to shut up about? I had no idea. That made no sense to me and it just looked like he was being a jerk for no reason.

In the car on the way back I asked why we could not go to Aaron's apartment and Dad nicely said he did not think we were invited. Phil jumped in with some jerk statements about that being why he'd told me to shut up, and then I just felt like crummy garbage as usual around Philip.

Tenth Grade
Age Fifteen

In my tenth-grade year I became lonely. I kept thinking that if I had a boyfriend all of my problems would be solved. I needed to be hugged. I needed someone to love me. My friends knew I was gay — only my closer friends, up until then. No problems were created by them. Those that knew didn't cause problems about it. I had no reason to believe anyone would.

I did what I thought could solve my issue of loneliness. I asked three girls if they knew any gay guys, and talked about how much I wanted a boyfriend. They acted like a guy they knew was gay, who actually wasn't, and went up to these dangerous-looking Mexicans to supposedly hook me up with their friend Roman.

In no time people were yelling slurs at me between every class. It was more than a few people, every single time I needed to get to class. I always knew what they looked like. I always knew what they would say. It was horrible and I didn't know how to get it to stop. I didn't want to be violent. I also didn't want lots of Mexicans to come after me or my brothers when they would come to that school later. I was just completely stuck. I put up with so much nonsense and wasn't sure what to do. The only time one of those incidents was reported was when my friend Richard and I had a falling out and he yelled things at me. I told Mom and Dad and my Dad had me bring a letter to school. It turned out that Richard got suspended, but things only got worse from him after that and his friends started to not like me either, even though it wasn't even my idea. This turned out so poorly I never wanted to tell on anyone else about bullying again.

However, the teachers did know. At one point I was harassed in my history class and my teacher just talked to me after class to let me know it was harassment. She wasn't sure what to do. No one was. It was out of control. My friend Manuel told me that if I fought someone, people would have respect for me. It just wasn't in my nature to do that, not to mention people were kicked out of school for only one fight. It did not seem like a good idea for a lot of reasons, and did I really want to get kicked out of a second school? How would that look on my record?

It was in my tenth-grade year that my Asperger symptoms got completely out of control, and it became worse during this time of harassment. My mood swings became completely bipolar. I had big ups and big downs and would get depressed and have suicidal thoughts.

I started to spend a lot of time alone reading. My Mom told me once how reading was like going into another world. Suddenly that didn't seem like such a bad idea. So I read library books, and hung out alone a lot, and started filling up journals to make sense of my thoughts.

When I did hang out with people, I floated around between people that I knew. I liked being polite and nice to people, and didn't want to burn bridges with people that I knew. I was building a network of friends and acquaintances, people to at least have lunch with, and it was nice. It was a transitional time for me, and there were definitely good things about this year. It's too bad it can be plagued by bad memories of rotten apples when there were plenty of good things too, even if they are harder to remember sometimes. With this out-of-control bullying situation, there were enemies, but there were allies as well, and people who didn't like that it was happening.

With my Asperger symptoms, not only were my mood swings all over the place, but along with that came a bad sleeping schedule where I slept all over the place as well. Being obsessive about weird things, social-skill problems — all kinds of stuff suddenly was at an all-time high. The symptoms just went manic, through the roof. The worst thing was that I had these non-stop pounding thoughts over and over again. I thought to myself if I couldn't get them to slow down I'd have to put a bullet in my head. It was torture. I couldn't slow it down.

My social skills became off-and-on again. I told my friend how I wanted to hug him, and he stopped being friends with me. I didn't know how to say things or do things right. I just had my own little world, my own way of looking at things or saying things, and it just didn't work with other people at times. I hated when I made someone uncomfortable by accident, but it happened sometimes.

All of these problems were at an all-time high when I began seeing the counselor, Lisa. She helped in some ways, but I also felt she was too quiet and wasn't offering enough feedback. I wanted to see someone else but my parents wanted to keep me with her. Philip started bugging me out of nowhere talking to me about "do you know how much Mom and Dad pay for counseling?" It wasn't something that was on my radar to think about.

How low can anyone get? I had a nightmare of symptoms happening along with the harassment, and Philip makes a point of insulting me for how much it cost to sort it out. I asked Mom how much it cost and Mom wouldn't tell me, only to tell me in an outburst later that it was eighty dollars an hour. That seemed like far too much suddenly. I also felt pressured to make more progress than I was making. So I called Lisa and let her know I was going to stop counseling.

At school the harassment was getting severe enough that I started cutting my fifth- and sixth-period classes to hang out with my friend Manuel. I didn't like going to those classes because I was sick of the rude stuff that was happening around me and didn't feel like I could deal with it any further, so I went on long walks with my friend. For my math final I drew pictures on a paper and did not turn in a test since I didn't know anything anyway. I took Fs for both the classes and didn't care one bit. It was hard to care about anything anymore.

Dad was picking me up after finals that day and the harassment had gotten so severe I said:

"Dad I need to switch schools for next semester."

"Okay."

Yet after the weekend I was taken to school as if that conversation never happened. Any rational parent would have pulled me from school but my parents didn't. It seemed he only said "okay" to be done with the conversation. He didn't actually want to do anything about it. Then the following semester harassment continued to get worse.

I passed the proficiency test so I could go to college when I wanted, but Dad insisted I keep going to this school, despite all these problems, so that I had something to do. He didn't want me staying at home all day.

I started to get punished for my bad grades and Mom and Dad thought that "pushing me in the right direction" by taking away TV privileges and other privileges would accomplish that. It didn't. I just got more depressed and resentful.

It was in the middle of all this stuff that my Dad told me at the end of an argument about gay people, "Besides, it's a sin!" and I responded that I didn't believe in his garbage religion and I hated that he made us go to church growing up. Soon after that, Dad nicely told me that they were taking me to an "educational seminar." It didn't seem like a bad idea. I didn't even know what that would be like at all. Before going, though, my parents and I weren't getting along and I tried to back out. Spending a weekend together seemed like a bad idea. Dad got mad because I went against this "plan" that he had. This seemed suspicious. Dad made a good living as a lawyer and this didn't seem to be about the money.

We showed up and there were picketers outside saying things like, "We're here! We're queer! We refuse to live in fear!" We went inside and the seminar started. This "educational" seminar felt a lot like crawling into a hole and dying. It told me all about how if I was gay I was going to live a depressing and terrible life, and how gays all cheat on each other. It followed every bad stereotype and every made-up thing about gay people imaginable and preached it like it was fact. It felt absolutely horrible to listen to it for the hour or so before I joined the picketers and spent all day with them. I even made a one-day boyfriend. Paul and I tried to keep it going, but with living two hours away from each other, it dissolved quickly before I could see him again.

Mom and Dad were disappointed the weekend hadn't turned out how they hoped, but they didn't try to do that again. When I confronted Mom about it later she denied it was an "anti-gay seminar." Dad never admitted that was what it was. I hardened against my parents. I felt bad about how I'd treated them before, when I was bad to them, but suddenly I no longer did. They no longer just felt like the enemy. They were the enemy. They had attacked me about my sexuality in a way so messed up I could hardly believe it, tricking me into attending that nonsense.

My depression started to spiral out of control. Suicidal thoughts pounded my head frequently for the rest of the school year. I cut myself up once but was never brave enough to go further, but I thought about death all the time. I couldn't get it out of my head. The harassers at school seemed to want it. My parents thought being gay was wrong and my family couldn't even talk to me about it unless it was in some weird way. Everything seemed to point to being better off without my life.

My symptoms stayed out of control, although sometimes medication helped balance things a little. Sometimes I would forget a pill and would get depressed. My Dad kept asking, in front of family members, "Did you take your pill?" every day even though I kept asking him not to. I hated the idea that anyone would ask me about it. I didn't want anyone to know I was chemically unbalanced. It seemed weird. Even a church lady randomly asked me about it at a church retreat because my parents told her to, and it was in front of friends. She tried to ask sort of quietly, but they heard it.

People showed concern in weird ways, like my Grandma (on Dad's side). After I missed my sister Erin's wedding, (and this was after I asked Mom and Dad not to tell her why I was not there but they ignored this and told her anyway), I got these weird letters saying, "Your name was brought in front of the church in prayer." They had more than twenty signatures of church members on it. I got these a couple times but they stopped when Mom told Grandma I did not like it.

One day I had an interview at Glendale Community College. Before we began our drive I got mad at Mom for being so late coming out to the car for something so important, and she told me terrible things for the rest of the way there, starting with, that I wanted everyone to feel sorry for me and that no one does. I tried to hold myself together, but couldn't, and when we arrived I spoke to my interview lady alone. I could not control my emotions and started crying. I told her about the situation and she said she'd "recommend me to a general placement." We concluded our conversation and I walked out, and Mom went in for a one-on-one conversation. When I asked Mom about the general placement afterwards, she said that they had not talked about it, which I found suspicious and was skeptical about that.

This conversation led to my Dad looking up a boarding school and finding Freedom Mountain Academy. This school was ten thousand dollars for one year and at the end of the year they would give me one thousand dollars back. It was a school that charged less because of farm work involved. I knew nothing about it, didn't even read the packet, but I was all in.

When summer came the fighting with my parents got awkward. One of the things that confused me about Mom then was how she would act like going to Washington was a choice and when I said I didn't want to go she'd guilt us into going somehow anyway, but then later would act like I didn't have to go if I didn't want to. She never would say what she meant. So when I did make a big deal about not wanting to go, to make it obvious I didn't want to, to try to get her to tell the truth and admit I had no choice, it just made both of us mad instead. She never could say what she meant about that, but I didn't have a choice, and she could never be straightforward about it. She would teeter-totter around and act like it was my choice when it wasn't. She didn't know how to say what she meant, and for a literal person with Asperger's, this was insanely confusing. This was one of our causes for fights at this time.

I know I was unpleasant, but it's not that I necessarily meant to be. Things were genuinely confusing, I was angry, and had so many issues just mounting up. I needed a release of them somehow, and counseling seemed to not be in the equation anymore for some time. Although we did have a few summer sessions with a new woman in Washington. At one point she told Mom to stop bothering me about my grades, but Mom told me she wasn't going to listen to her.

I had planned on going to Pasadena City College. I asked Dad about the deadline and he said, "Oh. You missed it."

"I missed it and you didn't tell me?!"

"Your education is your responsibility; don't you blame me for your problems!"

I got upset and left the room. Didn't Dad understand I didn't know a thing about starting college? I thought I was going to be backed up and get his help with this. It was not even true, either; I did not "miss" anything. I could have "added" the classes, but, gullible me, I took what Dad said at face value, but it taught me a valuable lesson. For important things, double check, always. Although two years would have been too much to skip of high school anyway.

As far as I knew, college did not work out, and instead of pursuing another community college, and there were other ones not too far, as I would find out much later, boarding school just seemed like the only option. It wasn't just about education anymore. Being away from family seemed like the only option. I knew I was self-destructing and I didn't want my family to be around it anymore.

My brothers seemed to hate me, and just thought I was a jerk. I don't entirely blame them but I did wish they had more insight about what was actually going on instead of altogether blaming me. In a family where Autism was never talked about, where Asperger's and disabilities were never a topic of conversation, they had limited understanding.

Aside from Mom reading something that sounded like I had symptoms matching Asperger's when I was nine there was never a diagnosis, never a plan to help. It never became a family issue. I didn't know all the problems I had were Asperger symptoms that kept whirling through my head. I just thought I was weird and had bad problems.

My family just thought I was a jerk. There were no answers, the symptoms were not looked into, and there were not many books at the time. Much later a lot of Asperger books would come out, but knowledge was more limited, and sending me to a specialist or anything like that was never talked about as far as I knew.

Whether they were too lazy or just did not want to pay for it, who knows, but it just never felt like a concern to my parents. Instead they had a lot of books like Parents' Guide to Preventing Homosexuality by Joseph & Linda Ames Nicolosi on their bookshelves. They read those books. They read books for fun. They had books about Asperger's but if they had read them their understanding of it would not have been so limited. I don't believe they were ever read. I had no reason to believe they were.

However, they did follow, step by step, what the anti-gay Christian books and the anti-gay seminar said about preventing homosexuality. They even prevented me from learning to drive. Dad said I had to get good grades and make him trust me first. I wasn't fooled. I knew this wouldn't work and he was buying time. My being gay and being able to drive myself was out of the question.

9/11 happened the day I was supposed to fly to boarding school, and no planes were flying, so we drove across the country to Tennessee instead. We drove to this big hilly farmland with a lot of land, trees, and a huge house. It had a fence with a goat and a pig, with another fence for chickens. I didn't know what to expect, but hoped to find myself at my temporary home.

Eleventh Grade
Age Sixteen

At the beginning of the year nobody knew anybody and everyone seemed super nice. It seemed like everybody was going to get along great. Considering the recent problems I'd had at my last school I had no plans of telling anyone I was gay. It just seemed like anytime I told anyone, it created a nightmare of unnecessary problems, so I had no intention of bothering to inform anyone.

I went to sleep my first night, and the following morning when I was in the shower I saw a dark figure to my left in my peripheral vision. I had no idea who it was, or what I was supposed to do in this situation. Eventually, somehow, we started a conversation. His name was Kavaughn and he was the second-to-last person to show up, and had arrived that morning.

Pretty soon we went on an expedition that we began packing for. Our expeditions were between five and eight days. We packed our tents, food, sleeping bags, everything we needed in large packs. The hike was the most physically exhausting thing I had ever done. It seemed like my shoulders might have been too bony or lacking muscle. When we stopped for the night, they ached terribly whenever they moved. On the next month's expedition I no longer had this problem.

Having nobody to talk to about gay stuff, it seemed like writing in my journal was a good idea. I also thought I could remember what I wrote on a page. Samantha was curious and wanted to read a page out loud. Being sure that I remembered no gay content on that page, I went ahead and let her. Bob and Samantha were sitting around a campfire area with me, and Samantha read aloud what I'd written about Bob: "At first I thought he was—" she stopped speaking there and started laughing. The next word was "cute" but she didn't say it out loud.

A recurring theme with my Asperger's is not thinking that something I write down will get me in trouble, and it happened a lot. Mom told me that if you don't want the world to see it, then don't write it down. This seemed impossible advice to take at the time. I needed a place to open up and I used my journal for that.

The other recurring theme was difficulty saying "no" to people. For some reason that seemed rude and I couldn't do that. I got better at doing that in my adulthood, but when I was young it just seemed impolite to say "no" and it seemed impossible to do. In my family the word "no" seemed to mean that someone would push until they got their way, so that didn't help. It never seemed like an effective word.

Samantha and Bob walked down the hill, and I hoped they would keep what happened between us a secret. But suddenly Kavaughn was screaming. He ended up coming up to me when I sat by myself with his loser lapdog Chris walking with him. He yelled at me about how he should beat me up and how I "should have just told him." Nobody was in agreement with him. Everyone agreed that telling someone they are gay when they are naked in the shower was not the ideal place.

Kavaughn's reaction was terrible and this prompted Samantha to lie and say to people that she was not part of it and it was all Bob. Samantha made up wild stories and people caught on to that fast. Kavaughn apologized to me in front of a group of people to get his reputation back. It was totally fake, but people believed it with no problems.

Since it was our first expedition our leader, Kevin Cullinane, allowed us to have groups for starting fires. I had never learned how to make one, and the expedition ended and we went back home.

It was established before getting to the school that if we were to stay there we needed to be trusted. If they could not trust us, we would be sent home. This was not a bluff, and everyone knew it. It had already happened within the first expedition with a guy named Ethan who tried to run away. It was a clear threat. He didn't even make it three days.

We were all having free time on a Saturday when it became known that four of the seventeen students had snuck into town a couple miles away, come back, and gotten caught by Kevin's son Tim while Kevin was away for a few days on some kind of speaking trip. Tim said to them, "I've seen you. No need hiding it now."

They were sent to their rooms for the day and no one knew what would happen. Girls were crying over and over. It was an upsetting situation to everyone. Word came down from Kevin what kind of punishment they would receive. They would be sent home, and that would be the end of that.

This included a storytelling liar, Stefan, the jerk Kavaughn, his following lapdog Chris, and a girl who was believed to be a psychotic liar, Allison. It seemed sad at the time, but we moved on. Later we lost one more, Jimmy, who was constantly in trouble for his anger problems, and when he got caught shoving Nick he was sent home as well. The troublemakers were gone and we were all happier for it, even if we didn't want to admit it at the time; the mood visibly improved.

My brain still felt sick, though. I couldn't shake the depression and hurt that I felt from the previous year at my other school. One day I was on an expedition and woke up earlier than anybody else. It was a beautiful misty morning, and we were at the top of a grassy hill. I walked down these grassy hills and found a spot to be alone for a bit.

I wasn't sure what religion I belonged to. I was brought up Christian with church being mandatory but wasn't sure what I believed in, but I did pray. I sat down and prayed and prayed that God would take the sickness out of my head. I needed to stop being depressed and just be happy with my life.

I don't want to convince anyone that doesn't believe in prayer that prayer works, although it did work for me. I made a conscious decision to be happy, and the sickness of depression that clouded my head seemed to go away. I decided I would make sure to have fun the rest of the year, and people quickly noticed a dramatic change in my attitude and started to like and enjoy me a lot more. It was a great feeling. My farm work picked up a lot of speed, too.

A lot of the rest of the year was fun and social. There was a lot of enjoyable farm work and free time, but it didn't stop me from being accidentally weird once in a while. There were social cues and other things I got to figure out a little along the way. It was helpful being one of twelve students for the majority of the year (we started with seventeen, lost six, and a girl named Justyn was added in November). It made me understand myself and people a lot more than I had before I went there. There was lots of time for self-reflection. There were many times people were okay to tell me I was weird in both a good and a bad way. There were lots of things to update and change as I went on.

Asperger's: A Literal Journey

One thing toward the beginning was how, without realizing it or meaning to, I accidentally freaked Chris out. I was pacing around the house on our large main floor over and over, and didn't even realize I was doing that. Best to take a walk in those situations. He was in his room with Dan and loudly told me to go away. Dan told me later how Chris told him that had scared him.

Also early in the year, I had forgotten to shower for a few days and people were telling me that I was stinky. I honestly thought they were kidding. Things like showering or putting on deodorant just didn't make sense at the beginning of the year to me. I was too depressed at first to make simple connections like that. After enough complaints I finally started with the daily showers and deodorant. With enough people, including our main leader's wife, Patricia, telling me, I knew it wasn't people pulling my leg.

The most frustrating time I had at boarding school was when, at the beginning, we were no longer allowed to have group fires, and we had to learn to build fires on our own. I was put with Kevin Rae as my tent partner, and neither of us knew how to do it.

Our leader Kevin was "old school" and just saw things in his weird military way, through distorted lenses at times. He was of the belief that everybody could learn to make a fire just trying it by themselves. This did not work for "Little Kevin" and me at all. We were frustrated, trying and trying, over and over again. We tried anything we could think of for a couple of hours. It didn't work. We lied one time, saying that we started one, to get them off our backs. Not too long after that I came back to the tent and Little Kevin had started a fire, and from then on Little Kevin started to make them on his own.

Since I could never figure it out, I cheated. I went into town and purchased the big long lighters that they had. I made myself useful by getting many of those, candles, and other things to help start fires. I never once started a fire throughout the whole year by myself, and for some reason nobody seemed to catch on to this. They liked my usefulness with the equipment I made sure to have.

To be fair, "Big Kevin" didn't know that I had Asperger's. It's not something me or my family talked about, and there would be no way or reason for him to know. Things that were hard for me to understand remained mysterious, as I seemed intelligent but there were so many social cues and other things I did not understand.

It is important to me that teachers understand that people do not all learn the same way. Perhaps a hundred people can learn to start a fire by themselves, and only one of those would need to actually be taught. I tried getting Big Kevin to tell me how to do it and he said that I was trying to get him to do it for me. I told him I wasn't I just wanted to know how to do it, and he told us how Samantha and Betsy could do it, and how we were "ACTING LIKE CHILDREN!!". No one was allowed to help us learn. We needed to learn by ourselves. It was the most frustrating learning experience I ever had, and cheating my way out of it seemed like the only option.

One day I somehow felt comfortable telling Justyn about my frustration with this and she right away agreed that people learned in different ways. Being homeschooled, she understood this better. She let me know that she put a big log on the fire and how that would burn for hours. I felt better knowing how someone understood this. Justyn was a nice girl.

My OCD traits were strange in my boarding school year, as well. Girls teased me once about how I had random words written on my arm. I didn't stop my journal writing and I had a strong urge to write random words on my hand to remind me of things I wanted to write about, or weird random stuff on the side of my notes in class. I'd randomly remember presents I got from different birthdays, different memories I had, and I kept writing a couple words of different things to remember them. I did this over and over again. I also made notes in my books of different kinds, and it would bother me not to do it. It made reading a long pain in the butt, too, until I eventually quit doing it years later.

I went home from boarding school and saw my family for our two week Christmas vacation. It just felt weird and awkward to me, and I didn't say a whole lot apart from the first dinner, where Philip kept trying to steal the spotlight and make the story about him making jokes somehow. He seemed jealous that I had the "seat of honor," as my Dad called it when he had me sit there. I still felt hurt about things with family. Since we weren't an apologizing family I didn't apologize, nor see the need to, and my parents never did either. Things just stayed whatever they were between us, and in two weeks I went back to boarding school.

Things were confusing with Asperger's, and I admit I was defensive and needed to find "someone to blame" a lot. This was something that would change with time. I learned to be more responsible, I learned to word things better, but I wasn't there yet. Somehow I felt in my confusion that sending me back to boarding school in January was somehow a jerk move from my parents when it was not. I told my Dad some things about how unhappy I was, and he acted like he was listening and went along with sending me back. I didn't feel supported. So much felt unsaid right then.

The first every-other-Saturday town trip arrived, and I called my family like I always did. Nobody answered. I found out in a letter that Philip had been on the phone with our older sister Erin and that's why he didn't answer the other line.

Somehow I lost all motivation to call my family. I didn't like them. I didn't have anything nice to say to them or about them. They couldn't even answer when I called them on the phone, when I only had a 4-hour block of time for that once every 2 weeks. I spent the next three months not calling Mom without a clear reason except just not feeling like it or not being in the habit. One day Kevin's wife Patricia let me know that Mom had called because "apparently she has not talked to you since Christmas break." Patricia wanted me to call.

One day I did call and Dad answered the phone. We talked for a bit, since Mom wasn't home. I don't think my Dad remembered to tell Mom about it. Mom was hurt and not happy with me about not speaking with her. I never meant to hurt her like that. I just didn't feel like I had anything good to say. We had also had an unpleasant phone call where I was yelling and crying in November before Christmas break, which may have encouraged this a bit.

It is sometimes said about insomnia that when we can't sleep it is because something is bothering us. It never felt like a coincidence that this was happening during the January to April three-month stretch of school before our two-week spring break at home, the same stretch of time I didn't make a single phone call home until I called Dad at the end of the three months.

Suddenly I was having horrible sleeping problems, and they were much worse than anything I'd ever had. I could only sleep a full night every other night. The bad nights I was lucky to sleep a couple hours, sometimes nothing at all. I passed time doing pushups or sit ups, or having weird long conversations with myself, where the thoughts in my head were a person and my voice out loud seemed like a separate person. Rapidly analyzing in a manic state, over and over again. I couldn't walk much, except to the bathroom, or I would get in trouble with our leader Kevin, who slept in the floor underneath us, which looked more like a normal house.

At one point we started getting a punishment of spending a week in our rooms, except for the times we had to be outside for chores if we couldn't pay attention in class. Kevin made a point of mentioning to the class once, "Now, with David I have a problem. David likes spending time by himself. Have you guys all noticed that?" The class made some "yup" sounds and some general agreement. I hadn't realized this had been so obvious. I did get in trouble for not being able to pay attention in class once. When tested, I couldn't repeat something Kevin said back to him. I took my punishment. I had no issues with it whatsoever.

Over the year I felt that Bob was my closest friend, and one day we finally were alone and talked about how hurt I had been by him at the beginning of the year. He had outed me to everyone, according to two sources, even before the first expedition. It was strange to me that he would treat me like his closest friend after that, after deliberately spreading harmful things about me at the beginning. It wasn't something I could overlook. He genuinely felt bad about that.

In an earlier conversation with Bob I'd said something about how people weren't going to like me if they knew I was gay. He told me about how he had thought about me saying that, and went through every person and realized all of them liked me and had said different nice things about me. It was a tremendous ego lifter. It turned out that telling people the truth and having fun paid off. People turned out to have tremendous respect for me. Even "Big Kevin" told me at one point how much respect people had for me. He thought it was because I was "gentle."

When the year was over, girls cried, and my Dad, Grandma, and my sister Erin went to my graduation. Kevin asked my Dad if he was David's father. When Dad said that he was, Kevin told him, "There's a good mind on that one."

Patricia privately told me that Kevin had told her how he had considered giving me another year. If they did that then it was free, since that was how it was with this one-year program.

This was a nice offer and I appreciated it; however, it was clear to me, and I think to Kevin too, that I was looking forward to the next phase of my life, which was starting college a year early.

He also told Patricia: "If there is one kid I'd hate to see go, it's him."

Then all of us returned to where we came from.

Pasadena City College

Starting at Pasadena City College a year early after passing the proficiency test was a bit scary at first. I was the youngest person there from what I could see, and I wasn't sure how to start going about making friends or trying to fit in anywhere. I was pretty uncomfortable being in the position I was in. I had known eleven other students extremely well in close quarters for a school year, and now I'd moved back home with a school switch and knew nobody.

One day I was walking to a class and from out of nowhere I heard a girl.

"Hey."

I kept walking, feeling sure she was not talking to me.

"Hey."

I continued to keep walking.

A pretty blond girl jumped in front of me.

"Hey!"

Her name was Ally. She introduced herself to me. She was from the Los Angeles Church of Christ along with a guy who was next to her. It was a church in Glendale. I didn't know much about that church but felt I had heard mixed things about it. As the new kid at school, I was thrilled for anyone to be talking to me.

I immediately started going and saw that they were an active church, and they didn't just have their Sunday services but a number of "midweeks" as well. It felt nice to be included in things and since I didn't have a driver's license there were always people willing to give me rides home at no cost.

We had "studies" where a couple of them would sit me down and go over different studies of their text. It was divided into five types of lectures. I never asked for one; they just started doing it, and assumed I wanted to go along with it. I wasn't even sure what it was or what was going on.

There was one I did with someone else I met, Victor, called "The Darkness Study" and in it I was asked a series of questions. One question he eventually got to was "Do you struggle with homosexuality?" I paused and said, "We're skipping that question." He told me that we were not skipping that question. He talked about something else for a minute and came back to it. I refused to talk about it. He kept coming back to it and finally I caved.

I just felt so defeated. I hadn't wanted to talk about it. At Eagle Rock High when I told people I was gay it was a total nightmare of harassment. At boarding school I was mistreated as well, but fortunately those guys were sent home in the first couple months. It just seemed that whenever I talked about it, it was going to create problems. I never wanted to talk about it again.

I had a strange lack of ability to lie at the time, so I caved and I did talk to him about it. He rubbed my shoulders and told me how it was going to be okay. He walked away as I thought to myself how I could trust him and it would be okay, although part of me knew better. I had so much repressed anger about past experiences I wasn't sure how to make peace with. Victor moved away, and my secret with him.

Later we had a Vegas trip that a lot of us went on, that Victor returned for as well. I had a great time, but at one point in private I asked Victor if he had told anyone. "I told Rick," he said. My mind was blown and I felt so betrayed. I thought back to the times I had been around Rick, the speaker, and how awkward he seemed around me and how that hadn't made sense to me.

Victor had opened a Pandora's box I wasn't ready to revisit yet. Rick didn't tell anyone as far as I knew, but it didn't matter. They were forcing me to talk about and relive things I just didn't want to talk about anymore.

One day Mom was bringing me to school. I did something I did not do often, and thought about what it must feel like to be Mom right then. Here I was, all awkward and shy and depressed. I started to become concerned that she might feel it was because of her and that I didn't like her.

I let Mom know what had been happening and just concluded with that if she thought I was acting strange because of her I just wanted her to know that there was something else going on. Mom burst with compassion and let me know how sorry she was that all of that had happened and how awful it was.

All of the anger and defensiveness I felt in Eagle Rock High was still with me somewhat but less, and in boarding school I wasn't on great speaking terms with my parents either, but this seemed like the pivotal moment in those years where I was able to talk to my Mom again. I started to find that I could ask her for advice about social situations. For instance: how long was I to wait if someone wasn't showing up for a hangout? I would just wait and wait for an hour, and Mom told me that fifteen minutes was good. Then, if they asked where I was, I could say "I waited for fifteen minutes." Little things like this needed explanations for me sometimes, and it was nice to know I could come to Mom.

At the Los Angeles Church of Christ I made it known to a leader, Mike, who was putting me into the process of getting baptized, that I had issues with Rick. Mike spoke to Rick and gave me excuses for Rick about how the church wasn't perfect. He wanted to act like they were trying to help me. I screamed back, "How does this help me?! Rick hasn't once talked to me about it. How could it possibly help me that he knows?!"

"Wow, it's clear you're pretty angry about this." Mike changed the subject.

I had let my thoughts be known of why I couldn't return there anymore, and I left. Many people, including two friends of mine, were hurt by this church. They both called me frequently to vent about it for a while. They didn't like what they saw about my experience either. We did our best to put it behind us.

There were things at the beginning of the year that could be puzzling for me with the teachers at school at times, and I felt I did my best, but weird misunderstandings sometimes got the better of me. Looking back, it was clear that teachers should have been told that I had Asperger's, and maybe sometimes they wouldn't have been as hard on me. I didn't mean to do wrong, even though sometimes it may have appeared that way.

I had a math class where we had a test and everyone had blue books, which are standardized packets of paper. I didn't have one and I didn't know what they were and continued to just use blank paper. I took it up to the teacher. "THIS TIME I WILL ACCEPT IT," he said, "BUT NEXT TIME, I WON'T ACCEPT IT!"

I was scared and hurt. Where had that come from? I made sure to check the syllabus, and clearly it stated that we needed to use blue books for tests. How had I not heard the teacher say that? He must have said it in class, and somehow I did not hear that part. I didn't make that mistake again.

While I was part of the Los Angeles Church of Christ, joining the gay club, which was called United Rainbow Alliance, just seemed like a bad idea. I hadn't been sure what to do about it when I left the church either. One day I peeked my head in, but was too chicken to come inside and I left. I finally mustered the courage to come in a couple weeks later. A guy named Percy started talking to me and was friendly, and introduced me to Marcel. People were nice right away.

This came to be the point in my college time when I started to branch out. Socializing and meeting new people came frequently then, and kept happening until it was time to leave Pasadena City College. Sometimes joining the right club can give us roots to grow on, and I spent less and less time at home.

Mom and Dad wondered when I would get a job, and I wanted one but was afraid to get one. I just felt like I would fail somehow if I had one. With my social skills needing work, how would I do well at a job? Not being able to get a license to drive to work did not help my motivation either.

I continued to go to church at Christian Assembly in Eagle Rock, and felt like my active social life took priority over any money-making from a job. It would seem foolish later, but at the time socializing felt like it was my job. After so many times switching schools, actually laying down some roots and meeting people over my four years at school felt good. I learned how to socialize better and talk to people every day. I came a long way from the tenth-grade version of myself who couldn't come to a third meeting of the swim team because talking to people in groups completely freaked me out. My social anxiety was just so bad back then and it made me nonfunctional in situations.

I still had some issues that I was sorting through, but I was making massive improvements. Early in my time at Pasadena City College, around age seventeen, people at Los Angeles Church of Christ gossiped about me being, or the possibility of my being, bipolar. It was no secret. I had crazy highs and lows. One day I was up in the sky with happiness and made sure to talk and joke around with people and had fun doing it. The next day I would be in the dumps all day with awful depressing thoughts as well as suicidal ones. I avoided people during those slumps.

It became severe enough one day that I finally decided to get back on medication, since I had been off since boarding school. I was afraid I would end up hurting myself during one of my downswings and it was time to take responsibility back by making sure I could get my moods stabilized.

One thing medication did not stabilize, though, was my laughing problem. This had developed while I was at boarding school and people learned to make jokes about it. Our leader Kevin said that I was reading their thoughts and it made me think of funny things. It was nice to have that kind of acceptance there but in the real world people were more weirded out by it.

I went to a casual, small, instrumental concert on campus with my friend Danny from the gay club. When I talked to Danny, he made some kind of mention of my laughing. I had no idea that I had been laughing. He found that funny and confusing. How could I have possibly not known? But that's how bad it was.

I had no idea what it was or what I should do about it. I never spoke to my parents or a therapist about it. I just felt like it was part of me and I tried not to let it happen. My thoughts would sometimes surprise me. I'd think of funny things suddenly, and it would happen so abruptly I'd bust up laughing. That or it would happen when my mind was somewhere else and I'd laugh and not be aware I was doing it.

So many things got better for me with my socializing, but some things, like my mood swings and my random laughing, had no explanation at all. I continued picking my skin and blackheads on my arms compulsively at boarding school. It was so difficult to stop. I fixated and OCD'd on every blackhead. I was able to stop that in college as well. By then my arms were all messed up with light-colored scar tissue. My friend Lamont mentioned using cocoa butter and when I tried it the scar tissue from all of my nail marks went away like magic, with extremely fast results. It looked 50% better in one day.

For how well I was doing at school it didn't seem like my family understood me at all. Some things would continue to be issues during this time. There was always some excuse not to help me drive so I could have a driver's license. I had no clue what was being avoided but couldn't shake the thought that somehow being gay was bad to my parents. Driving for fifteen minutes once every two weeks is not sufficient driving time and I could not get coordinated enough to learn, but made do with the bus or rides from parents and friends. It was humiliating at times, but I made it work.

While people had started to learn about and love my eccentricities at school, it seemed like my family turned a complete blind eye to me in an opposite way. One of my biggest regrets of my childhood was that my parents allowed my relationship with my older brother, Philip, to become so toxic. At some point when I was growing up they just got sick of disciplining him and just let a lot go. As long as it wasn't hitting, he could say whatever awful hurtful thing to me he wanted and it was supposed to be fine, because, in the words of Mom, he was "just talking."

This was nothing new. He had done this as far back as I could remember. Since I'd had lots of trouble in fourth grade with socializing, Philip made sure to tell me "You did" (something at school), "no wonder you don't have any friends!" over and over again. The most hurtful things that he could think of to say, he made sure to say them. After lots of power struggles and trying to talk to Philip when he clearly didn't have anything nice to say, there was no sense in trying to work anything out with him. I finally had given up. Talking to Philip was an enormous waste of time. He always had something horrible to say, and I can't even imagine how angry and insecure someone must be inside to say the things he would say.

Over and over again I would ask Mom to do something about something he said, and she would say, "Oh, he's just talking!" as if it was funny, and tossed it off. I tried working it out, I tried reasoning with him and my parents, over and over again. He would provoke, he would still say awful things as soon as we were near each other, so I did the only thing there was left to do.

I cut him out of my life. It was liberating, actually. He would come home for the weekend from his college, and I made sure to be out with friends, someplace else. After a few weekends of this, family members started begging me to spend time with him, but I wasn't having any of it. There was no more talking, no more trouble-making, no more hurt feelings, no more awful words; it just suddenly was not worth my time. And you know what? It felt good. I was glad to have that toxic energy out of my life, and I replaced it with positive people and experiences. People would tell me that he was my brother and I should try to make up with him. I let them know that if they knew how bad he was they would not be telling me that. "You don't understand, nothing good comes from being around him," I said.

It's important that parents in general listen, but especially if a kid has Asperger's or Autism. They may have a kid that habitually picks on the Autistic kid and it may become such a habit it just becomes second nature to them. It may also become second nature for the Autistic kid to just put up with it because nobody has any better ideas. That's what it was in my family, until I cut that piece of my life away. It was too late for family intervention at that point, and I did the only thing that made sense by getting rid of that person.

"Guy that hugs everybody"

It's been said about Autism that kids who have it, even young kids such as three-year-olds, do not like to be touched. It's supposed to feel as if their skin is on fire. There are differences with me with certain things, and one noteworthy one, to me, was how I craved physical contact an unusual amount, and at some points in my life this craving was at an all-time high.

For example, when I was going through my church phase and I church-hopped around a bit between two non-denominational Christian churches and my Los Angeles Church of Christ church, I couldn't make up my mind which I wanted to stick with, and I became someone who hugged instead of gave handshakes.

One memorable moment was when a guy didn't remember me and another guy said, "He's the guy that hugs everybody."

"Oh, the guy that hugs everybody, now I remember you!"

It was light and funny. Things were like that for a while. But, being a guy and having mild Autism, there were things that I could not put into words well, and one thing was that I was shy about asking for a hug. For a while I did something that I would not encourage doing, and that's just hugging the person and hoping they are okay with it. One guy shoved me, one guy kind of punched me a little, which I was not expecting. People are taken off guard and don't know how to respond. Ask, "Can I give you hugs?"

Or kind of put an arm out and see what they do. Those are better options. Personally, I like just asking better, but that took a while for me to grow comfortable enough to do.

David Marr

I've always been pretty cuddly though. Even as a kid I was affectionate, which Mom wrote in her journal at the time, and she read to me once. One day when Philip and I were little I said, "Come hewe" (I couldn't say my r's right), and I kissed him on the forehead and lay down, and he did the same to me and lay down, and we did this for twenty minutes.

Diagnosis at Twenty

Somehow when I was twenty years old, living at home, the idea came up between my parents that I should have a diagnosis at the hospital. Mom pressed for it and saw it as necessary; my Dad did not see how it would make any difference. It started being in the process and I got several voicemails from a woman saying to call her back. I was asked to never use my cell phone longer than a minute so the minutes did not go up, so I kept not calling her back because I did not feel I was able to yet. The woman left her final voicemail saying that if we did not call her back she would assume we were not interested. Mom told me that with something like that I could have made the phone call on the cell, so I should have asked, I guess. It was a literal misunderstanding. I was waiting until I could call from a landline; it seemed like more than a one-minute phone call.

The testing process was interesting. There were cards I was supposed to be able to put in order and make stories out of them. I came across one set where a larger pizza man was making a pizza. In one card he dropped it and it fell on his head, and it dangled all over it. I started laughing hysterically and could not stop. She immediately gave up and we went on to the next set.

Another weird thing that happened was when we addressed the subject of being "monotonous" I kept saying "monogamous." Each time I said "monogamous" instead of "monotonous" she would correct the word. I asked if I had been saying "monogamous" and she replied, "Several times."

I ended up with a huge packet from this diagnosis which I felt was sort of helpful and sort of not. One eye-opening part was that somehow she got the information that I was getting counseling help for a while when I was nine and my parents stopped because they felt the counseling was "hurting their relationship with David." I don't think that was something they told me. I don't remember asking to stop, either; I just remember for a brief time meeting with a guy who was writing everything I said down. It sounded to me like an excuse to not do it.

There were other parts she had for my history or my family history that were just flat wrong, and I did not like at all. I was not sure where she was getting her information from but a lot of it was just incorrect. It made it hard to take the report she wrote seriously. It was over, though, and my parents and I did not talk about it.

Speech Class

Speech class was one of the main factors that helped me get out of my shell at Pasadena City College. It helped me quickly learn to speak in front of people and I was grateful for it. It also seemed like the perfect class to get out of the way in a summer or winter session. It was not hard at all to speed through.

What I found with speech class is something I have found in other parts of my life where I have spoken in front of people: something I say is unintentionally funny sometimes and it gets a laugh. I don't know why, but it happens. It is fun when I can be naturally funny and it can improve the mood and the speech.

At one point I was about to give a speech and a goofy guy I knew held his hands, close to his chin, with his elbows on the desk. He gave me a big smile attempting to be polite and attentive. I needed to correct this immediately.

"Please don't look at me like that, dude, it's really distracting, you're going to mess me up."

People started laughing.

"Oh, sorry."

I continued my speech in a burst of confidence, and it went well. I ended up getting an A in the class.

Theater Arts Class

If there was one class that was helpful for me and my socializing, this was it. I wanted to learn more about acting as an interest but what I did not expect to happen was how good it would be for me. I went from being shy at the beginning of class to being a lot more outgoing, and the level of progress felt incredible.

My normal shy, reserved self transformed into a silly goofball that people liked, and I started to have a total blast talking to people on campus. Sometimes someone can just be a "people person" and enjoy talking to people more than most people do, and I feel that I became that, and people enjoyed talking to me as well.

I do regret just a little not volunteering for more of the volunteer exercises. I guess I got used to watching. Sometimes in life we need to break out of our comfort zone a bit. There was a girl, Abigail, who would always volunteer. We talked just a little; I got along with her. It was Abigail who taught me to use my strategy of highlighting things in pink to memorize lines, a trick I still use to this day. It was tremendously helpful.

Years later I bumped into her at a Starbucks and learned that her acting name is now Abby Wilde and that she'd had three seasons on the show Zoey 101 as a series regular. I was so proud of her, and still am. As for the others, I am not sure how far they got.

The most memorable part of the class was one exercise I had to do for an assignment. I kept pairing with people who ended up dropping the class. I got no penalty for that, but still needed to do the assignment. I wondered a way I could do it that would be different than the others, since by now we had seen the short scene so many times.

The final line of the scene was, "Maybe I should wear my tux." So I had an idea that I could at the last part open up my shirt and reveal I was wearing a fake-tux shirt. I thought this shirt was in my clothes but I looked through them and I couldn't find it. I asked Mom where it was and she found it for me. She was a real trooper, finding it for me at the last second. When we were about to drive away she ran it out to the car and gave it to me. I did not think to ask sooner, and should have.

It came time for the scene and I was wearing a button-down shirt with only the top and bottom buttons buttoned, and doing the scene with my friend Franco, whom I asked not to tell anyone about the scene. At the last second I put on a blond wig that was there, for no reason.

The scene was finishing and I said, "Maybe I should" (I undid a button and then made my shirt open wide at the same time as I said) "wear—my—tux!" Then I started flexing my muscles and the class was laughing hysterically. I had no idea they would find it so funny. When the class calmed down my teacher, Whitney Rydbeck, spoke up and said:

"That was definitely…one of the most interesting ones of that I have ever seen."

In-N-Out Burger

When it came time to find a job in college, somehow my parents had talked to Becky at In-N-Out Burger, and she told them, "I have pull," and said she could help me get a job. Although I did not know Becky super well I had gone to church with her some years by then, and we were in the same small Sunday class for many years, and to some capacity she could vouch for my character. There was a month or so delay as a couple people had just started, but pretty soon I was going forward again and filled out an application and soon had an interview. I was nervous and didn't feel like I did well in the interview, I should have had practice interviews, but despite this he called me and said he'd "go out on a limb and bring me on to orientation."

Work was so much different than anything else I had experienced. In some capacity I felt ready for it since I was good at doing chores around the house. This was like that in some ways, but at a faster pace. I soon found out that when you didn't know what to do next you needed to walk and act like you were going to do something; otherwise someone would say, "Why aren't you doing anything?" You had to always be busy, or at least appear that way while you thought of something else to do.

They started me on dining room, which was doing trash and cleaning off tables and filling up the drink-station supplies, and a few days later I got started on learning to take orders. At first it was frustrating and I didn't understand a thing. Order taking was tough at first but after a while I caught on to it.

I had an advantage that turned out to be a secret weapon. At home I was a fast typist and it impressed people who saw it. That coordination led me to being a rapid-fire order taker. It was great and people were happy with it and pretty soon I would have been perfect except for one thing: I couldn't smile to save my life. That's something that would develop better over the years, but at the time felt impossible. Fake smiling, even just a little bit, did not feel like something I could do. I was stone-faced, but I was fast.

After a few times of asking me to smile, managers stopped asking and that was that. Years later I could do that fine, but at the time I just couldn't. I did, however, attempt smiling at one point, but my manager, Craig, just told me that it was cheesy looking and I stopped. There is a way to do it just a little and I guess I could not figure it out. However, there were also times I hit it off with a customer and it was no problem, but that was more accidental than on purpose.

Having Asperger's sometimes means that you're not sure how to handle certain situations right or know what to do. Sometimes it would be time to yell, "Six meat down!" for orders that contained six or more patties. I usually could do it but sometimes there were too many distractions from the customers wanting to talk to me. Coworkers kept asking me to do it, but occasionally I'd slip, and then the coworkers got rude about it at one point, when they were sick of telling me. I was hurt, but made a point to be better after a manager let me know that it was a frustrating situation for the cooks at the grill.

Things started out smoothly at my job, but pretty soon this coworker, Luis, and I started to not get along well at all. He acted like I was stupid because I couldn't figure things out, and I made it clear I didn't want to talk to him at all, but he was persistent and kept trying to talk to me anyway. I also took a manager literally when he told me to ignore him at one point:

"Luis says I'm going to get fired soon, is that true?"

"No, it's not true, just ignore him."

That wasn't what he meant but I ignored him anyway, thinking that was what he meant, which caused further problems. He did not mean it literally, which was a confusing double meaning right then.

I waited too long to talk to management about it. I should have spoken about it sooner. He said awful things like "Don't listen to him, he's retarded" to a customer who wanted my help with something. Whenever I saw him walk in the door I would get an awful sinking feeling. Certain managers kept having a word with him and Craig told him to shut up over and over near me once when he was misbehaving. I thought it was weird he wasn't punished worse, but was grateful for the help. He was also known for coming into work drunk while managers looked the other way, and I think he misbehaved more during those times. He would soon be transferring to another location anyway.

I felt this was important to bring up because, if it's at all possible, it's good to work for a company that understands disabilities or puts people in positions that work for them. There were many jobs there, so there was bound to be one that worked for everyone. What there wasn't, though, was a decent system for write-ups or getting someone fired. Luis got away with much too much, and so did others. It just wasn't a place that fired people unless they did something outrageous, like give out free food. For that they would fire a person on the spot.

There were a couple memorable encounters with customers toward the beginning. I learned quickly that people found it rude if I made counting motions with my hand (which helped me think).

My coworker Justin told me not to do that, so I stopped. I made a motion for a customer to come forward with a finger and she nicely told me that it is a motion for a dog so she does not like that. I appreciated her feedback and never did it again.

Going through my interactions, I did not give a lot of thought to little things, like how I gave back a receipt. Without intending to I gave it too close to a customer's face once. I am not sure if I did it more times than that, but he made a big stink about it, wanted free food, which I could not even do with my order-taking system, wanted to talk to my manager, etc.

I overheard him say that I "acted annoyed with him," which was a bold-faced lie. I was nothing but concerned trying to figure out what I did, which he would not tell me. A manager referenced what it actually was at a meeting later. It just seemed like he jumped the gun to get free food, though, but I never made that mistake again. He even said while talking to a manager, "I deserve free food." How obnoxious.

The time I had there wasn't all bad, though, and Napoleon Dynamite was a movie that came out at the time, and since I reminded people of him with my weird monotone voice people wanted to call me Napoleon, and I let them. Pretty soon if people called me David I told them that wasn't my name and to call me Napoleon. I liked it a lot, although it might have alienated me a little, but it gave me an identity in the place.

There were a couple of new cooks that came in that were funny and silly. I enjoyed them. One day I was hyperactive and was singing the Whitney Houston song "I Wanna Dance With Somebody". It was late with no one around and I was near the order-taking machine. I sang, "I need a man to take the chance," (these are not the correct lyrics, by the way), and I realized a few things at the same time.

For one, I didn't know any more lyrics to the song. Next, I realized that I'd just sung out loud "I need a man" at a place where I'd never told anyone I was gay. Sure, they suspected, and it was easier for people to suspect with me at the time—the young aren't as well hidden with that—but I never talked about it. Lastly, I realized that Tony, the cook, was looking at me with this big goofy smile on his big chunky white face.

I marched right up to him with a fake tough guy look.

"Why are you looking at me like that? What? What are you looking at me like that for? What? What? Why are you smiling at me for? What? What? What?" I finally gave up. "I can sing to Whitney Houston if I want!"

I marched away like I had just settled a score. Tony was laughing and bowing his head like I had said the funniest thing he'd ever heard.

The next day I went to the break-room area and Tony and this other guy Johnny were there, standing up behind the chairs against the wall.

"Hey Daayviiiid," Johnny greeted me in a feminine fashion, like he was into me.

"Why are you talking like that?"

"This is how I normally talk Daviiiiid."

I started laughing and getting red-faced. I had to leave and come back for some reason and they were still standing like that when I got back. I got more red and started giggling trying to eat my food.

"What's so funny Daviiiiid?"

Someone else might have been insulted by this experience but I found it hilarious. In-N-Out was a Christian company though, and even if I did have a way to tell people I was gay I chose not to do it and tried to remain professional. That was advice Mom had given me before I started, and I chose to take it.

I liked my hyperactive nature at this time of my life, being twenty years old. I made up my mind that I was going to have fun at work, and not be bothered by the negativity of other people, so that's what I did.

There was one point where for some reason Craig fake-laughed at something I said in a rude way, so without missing a beat I fake-laughed back.

"Ha ha ha—ha ha ha—ha ha ha ha ha—uhhhhh—see how that feels!"

A bunch of guys around me laughed like I'd said the funniest thing ever, which I was not expecting. This kind of weird goofy stuff I did worked in my favor sometimes.

I had some good times there. Things changed around when we got a new manager. The manager, Gary, who'd hired me was replaced with this guy Kurt. Upon meeting Kurt he seemed friendly enough and I felt he would be a good manager, but things turned south quickly. He hired a bad English-speaking guy who quickly got promoted above some of us who had been there longer, promoting him for raises he did not earn since he could not learn the tasks the raises required learning. Learning to take orders was skipped, he got the raise for not learning it, and then he learned to do fries, when some of us had been wanting to learn fries to get that raise.

Things like that kept happening and the unfairness of the situation was a slap in the face every day. I had worked hard to get where I was but my hours had to be cut for school, and Kurt did not know how I'd worked hard that whole summer, as well as all the time I'd put in since then. Kurt knew none of that. Kurt only knew me from my reduced hours, which was a problem.

A friend offered me a job at Hollywood Video and I took it. I worked both positions, but not many days for either. For quite a while it was two days of Hollywood Video a week and only one day of In-N-Out Burger a week. I started to hate In-N-Out Burger and felt like I went to a dark emotional place for the one day a week I went there. The management changing around didn't agree with me one bit. I loved all the managers I'd started with, but the management switching became awfully problematic.

One new lady manager, yelled at me three different times because I didn't understand something fast enough and would ask a question, all within seven days. I called Human Resources on her and she got her act straightened out. I don't think people were friends with her enough for that to affect anything with retaliation (which is why I'd never called Human Resources on Luis). On a different day this manager, wanted to know who could go home because we had too many workers.

I offered and was on my way out. Right then a hungover employee who had had a birthday party the night before called sick. She asked me to come that night and I was too afraid to say no, or wasn't sure how to handle it. Since I didn't drive I walked the 2.1 miles home, took an hour or so nap, then walked all the way back to work. It was my least favorite workday of the whole time I worked there. I should have called and explained that I couldn't do it. I don't think she was aware that I did not drive, still being new to the position. Not being able to say no causes weird dilemmas with Asperger's at times, and this was one of those.

There was one repeated action that I did there that I regretted more than anything else at In-N-Out Burger, but I was too naïve, gullible, and impressionable a person to see the harm in it at the time. Here I was, working one day a week, already having once been told some time ago by Kurt that he didn't have a problem with workers doing it, just to make sure I worked that one day a week. I forgot about that for a long time.

Since at this job people were usually cut after 5-6 hour shifts, there would always be a swarm of girls asking if they could go home early, so I did too. I wanted to spend a minimum of time at the place I was starting to resent so much. I could have just quit except Dad felt I needed to "keep my foot in the door" and it seemed like a smart move to get a whole year on my resume. The thing was, I thought nothing of asking if I could leave early that one day a week. I thought it was the same as everyone else doing it.

What I know now that I didn't know at the time was just because they are not telling you to quit asking doesn't mean that they are okay with it. They might think you are an annoying pest. They may hate all of the girls that are doing it and just haven't told them, and I just joined them. Not to mention that the fact that I could only work one day a week at the time with school and Hollywood Video meant that I needed to stick my shift out and not ask.

I met Rob when he visited Los Angeles and we started dating, and a couple months later I would be moving to Vegas to be with him. I thought I could ask for more hours later but it didn't work out that way. About nine months later I attempted to get a job at another In-N-Out Burger and when Kurt was contacted he said, "He was an okay worker I guess," and the other guy jumped in and said, "He had other priorities while he was working here." My resentment of the place towards the end, and my constantly wanting to get out of there earlier had ramifications. I should have had a better attitude, but in my mind I was doing fine. It was hard to fake happy in that place after a while and it felt impossible to do, though.

There are many mistakes I made with my first job that I would never make again in a million years. My hope is that people can have compassion for people with Asperger's, or anyone else, and just note that sometimes things may have to be explained that you would not expect to have to explain. Some things were easy for me to put together. Some things were not.

"Things sound nicer when you smile"

In Vegas, I ended up working at a second In-N-Out Burger job, and I learned one valuable lesson there that I took with me from my manager, Christine, for the rest of my life.

At In-N-Out Burger when we have things ordered, say, three double doubles for example, with the math, that is six meat patties. For that we call out to the cooks, "Six meat down!"

This happened one day and I was told to smile when I said it, that it sounds nicer. I started smiling when I would say it, and it did sound nicer!

It is easy to overanalyze smiling. I felt like I could not do it on command; it just happened when it happened. It was hard for me to do at my first In-N-Out Burger, and I sort of stopped trying. I did not know how, and when I did, it was fake looking, and I was told to stop. Smiling "just a little so something sounds nicer" is far easier to manage, and actually has a reason that makes sense, and I have been doing it ever since when I need to speak to someone at work. Thanks, Christine, for the amazing life lesson. This has helped me tremendously.

Driver's License

When I was fifteen I was not the best kid, so I was not mad or surprised when my parents wanted to prevent me from getting my permit at that age. When I asked my Dad about getting a permit he said that I needed to get good grades, get my parents to trust me, and be nice to my parents in order to be able to do that. They would not sign off on it otherwise. Someone may look at these three things and say, "Well, just do it then." I knew better. This was a way of putting it off. I was gay and they wanted me on a tight leash. Even back then I had a feeling the driver's license thing would not happen no matter what I did.

The year I was at boarding school there was no need and no way to drive. Twelve students, including me, were on a big farm, with a humongous hill with a forest behind it, and none of us ever drove a car except our leader, Kevin. The driver's license idea was put off until the following year when I would be attending community college at Pasadena City College.

There were four years spent finishing my Associates of Arts/Science degree. There were many times when I thought I would fail a class and dropped it. Some of those I was right to drop, a couple maybe I wasn't. I dropped Intermediate Algebra over and over until I was not allowed to take it there again, I kept dropping it because I would not have passed no matter what I tried. That was a lot of wasted effort. This class could have been taken at an online school instead, and I should have done online school anyway due to my difficulty with taking tests and comprehension problems, as University of Phoenix did not do tests for my Bachelors in Psychology, except for my one Math class I needed, but I would learn all of this much later. The school route just didn't work, and online school also helps make hours available for jobs. In any case, it took that long to finish the degree and the driver's license battle between my parents and me was going on during this time.

At first maybe I liked taking the bus to go to school. I didn't see anything wrong with it. I made friends with those Los Angeles Church of Christ people, and there were always guys that drove us around and never asked for a lick of gas money. I should have offered.

It wasn't until later when I left that church and got into the United Rainbow Alliance, which was our gay club at school, where I became increasingly bitter about having to mooch rides off of friends. Sure, they were happy to do it most times, most people I knew, but I got sick of it pretty quickly. If I wanted to do anything, I would only be able to do it if a friend also wanted to do it and took us there. Not everyone is comfortable taking cash for gas money, but I do regret not at least offering to pay for meals here and there.

Looking back at my parents' actions around this time, it seemed like they were scared of something and not sure how to deal with it. I wonder if it was ideas that they heard in that anti-gay seminar (called "Love Won Out") or any of the weird anti-gay books they read that cast bad messages to them. They seemed to fear what I would do if I was able to drive.

At the time, though, I was a naïve and gullible person. If they said that I was a bad driver and that it would take forever for me to be able to learn to drive, I believed it. They helped me drive just enough to say that they were helping but not nearly enough to help me actually learn to drive. I was lucky to even be able to drive for fifteen minutes once every two weeks. I lacked coordination and should have been driving every day. I did not fully realize this, though. I thought not being able to learn was my fault, which is what they wanted me to believe.

At one point their excuses changed; they would let me drive but they would not pay insurance for it. Having to walk or take a bus to a job is embarrassing and it was demotivating, but I wish I had done it sooner anyway. If I could do it again I would have had a job all four of those years and paid for driver's training and gotten myself a car and insurance. I had been scared to death of getting a job and of not being able to do it with my Asperger's. I never told my parents that, though. I was looking for jobs, though unsuccessfully, but could have been looking more. Having to take buses to get there though was not exactly motivating; it was embarrassing, and there was no chance in sight of getting a license.

When Becky was going to help me get the In-N-Out job I was happy to start working. I worked all summer all the hours that they wanted me. Pretty soon I had saved up $7,000 dollars, but this ended up being a bad thing in a lot of ways. Suddenly my parents' excuses became increasingly obvious; they would not let me drive. They often claimed they were too tired — their favorite excuse. Although Mom was a few minutes away, sometimes she'd pick me up from school more than forty minutes late. I would look forward to driving home to Eagle Rock and getting fifteen minutes of driving in, but sometimes she drove all the way home without explanation.

I began to get furious sometimes, and cold with them other times, but nothing ever made a difference. There was one car ride with Mom and Dad where I asked to drive and Dad had some dismissive excuse for an answer, and I said, "Yeah there's always some excuse."

Mom and Dad gasped with surprise. It was actually meant to come out as a joke but it came out cold, and I did nothing to correct it. I let it hang in the air awkwardly.

I finally did a driver's training that didn't teach me anything, and the teachers were terrible. There were four sessions and I only did three because the teaching was so pointless, but also because I met Rob.

We talked a lot and had a couple visiting weekends and we wanted to move in together in Vegas where he lived. He assured me he would help me get my driver's license. I had a bad feeling about him, which I ignored because I was so desperate for a better life. He also assured me that he would work on his temper, and I wanted to believe him, against my better judgment. I felt trapped in this bubble living with my parents. There were so many opportunities for growth I would have once I was able to drive. As long as I was with my parents, it seemed it would never happen.

It was Rob who told me when he was learning to drive that you have to drive every day, and I realized I wasn't as much at fault for my lack of driving skills as I thought. All of my parents' evasiveness became apparent. There was a point in my time at Pasadena City College where I grew so sick of people asking me why I didn't have a driver's license that I wrote a blog on MySpace (which was what people used at the time before Facebook came along), explaining my parents' behavior. I made up my mind if anyone else asked why I wasn't driving, I would direct them to the blog, rather than have to repeat myself about this sore subject again. I must have had some idea that my parents' evasiveness was why my driving ability was not improving, as I made that blog, but it made more sense talking to Rob about it later.

When I was living in Vegas I once got a random voicemail from Mom telling me to be careful what I put on MySpace because employers could see it. I didn't have any idea where this had come from, and my blogs were marked "friends only" so employers couldn't see them anyway. In a later phone call she mentioned how what she was saying was that she had read my MySpace blog and I guess this was her way of telling me.

"And a lot of what you wrote was not truuuue. We did help you. For years!"

I suddenly erupted and couldn't hold it in anymore. All of the lies and evasiveness over all this time finally exploded.

"THAT'S JUST THE POINT MOOOM!! YOU WOULDN'T HAVE HAD TO HELP ME FOR YEEEARS IF YOU HAD HELPED ME A DECENT AMOUNT BUT YOU DIDN'T! YOU GUYS WENT OUT OF YOUR WAY TO NOT HELP ME! DO YOU HAVE ANY IDEA HOW MANY TIMES YOU WERE TOO *TIRED* TO LET ME DRIVE OR YOU WOULD DRIVE ALL THE WAY TO EAGLE ROCK AND NOT BOTHER TO PULL THE CAR OVER! I WAS LUCKY TO DRIVE ONCE A WEEK AND IT WASN'T ENOUGH TIME!"

"But you got to have that driver's training. We paid for half of that."

"I didn't even go back to that place for my fourth session because of how stupid that place was. Mom you went out of your way to —"

"Okay, okay, okay."

Mom had heard enough. When I visited Los Angeles not long after that, my parents gave me a check for $1,000 dollars for my Jeep, I was buying off Rob for $1,500. I was so stunned I was speechless. I don't know why my parents couldn't acknowledge some things, but it was the closest they would ever come to admitting their evasiveness, and excuses, for never teaching me to drive.

It also wasn't the same with the other boys. When my younger brother Stephen got close to his driver's license test date, my Dad said he had to help him learn to drive well so he wouldn't be able to help me drive for a while. This never happened with me, and I had gotten many permits and driver's tests.

I felt my parents were trying to protect me from being gay at the time. I hated them so much during that time though and I didn't think our relationship could ever recover. The whole driver's license issue was one more wedge between me and my family. My parents and I were feeling more and more like distant acquaintances. The love I had for them when I was young did not feel like it was coming back, and I felt more and more on my own.

I hope that people can help their children get a driver's license and not let being gay or having Asperger's be a reason to avoid it or make excuses about it, or make it the kid's fault that they can't drive better, like my parents did. It was a terribly confusing and frustrating experience I wouldn't wish on anyone. I felt dangerously close to casting my parents out of my life for good.

An Abusive Relationship

A fear I have with people with Asperger's is that they will settle for a bad relationship like I did for a year and a half. There were red flags early on before I even moved in that Rob had a temper, but I wanted to believe him when he told me that he would be better. This is a difficult, if not impossible, thing for someone to get better about, but he told me he would quit doing it, and I wanted to believe him. Even before we moved in together, there were things that made me feel bad, but I needed to start a new life and get a driver's license and get away from my overbearing parents, and my judgment was clouded. If it wasn't for my anger with my parents about the driver's license, I don't think I would have made the choice to move in with him, and I think I would have been smarter about it. My life was going to be so limited forever as long as I was not able to drive. Rob promised early on that he would help me learn. My life felt frozen with my parents. I did not feel I had a choice but to move in with him.

What I didn't know though was that learning to drive with Rob meant him screaming at me a lot, loudly, when he'd get impatient. It was awful, and my anger towards my parents for not helping me grew deeper. I'd start to shake with pain, and hurt, and make myself concentrate as it seemed like the only way that I would learn.

At first I tried to be nice to Rob in the relationship, but not too long into it I stopped caring as much and would loudly yell at him to get him to "SHUT UP!!" I didn't want to keep tolerating it, and I stopped feeling like I owed him something.

It is unfortunate that there are some people that are like this. They just seem to lash out and say rude stuff a lot, and it is always your fault that they are mad. It is never their problem that they get mad about every single thing.

Something that took me a long time to pinpoint with Rob is that he complained all of the time. For some reason I didn't notice this until late in the relationship, maybe a year in. One day it hit me: Hey! This guy complains about work when he's with me, complains about all the slow drivers in the car, complains to Mom about me when he isn't around me, and complains about me to his coworkers at work! Talk about someone who likes to complain!

I'm not sure what made him this kind of a person, but he had some kind of darkness inside of him, and he always manipulated me into staying with him when I wanted to break up. Once he told me it would cost me upwards of $3,000 if I did break up with him, to try to scare me into staying.

He's someone I have regretted introducing to my family, but what's done is done and I can't do anything about that. I wish my family had never met him. One day he told me, like he used to do often, how we should break up. It was his way of trying to get my attention, but I wasn't having any of it, so I left him after a year and a half together. Later he would sadly say, "Oh, we could have worked it out," so clearly he did not mean it.

I just worry that people with Asperger's could get caught in a relationship like this because some part of us may feel we deserve it, but we don't. Some part of us might want some negative feedback because other people won't tell us. I think part of me stayed with Rob for a year and a half because I felt like I deserved whatever he told me, because I wanted to learn to be more normal. Now I know I need to be with someone who accepts me for who I am. We can't always change personality traits for each other. These weren't things that could be worked out and quitting sooner should have been okay, but I was far too forgiving, and I gave far more second chances than what were deserved.

It seemed like Rob wanted me to feel trapped in a relationship with him, and feel like being with him was the best I could do. One hurtful thing he did over and over was tell me, "good luck finding someone who would put up with all of your nonsense". It seemed like a control-freak move, since according to him I would be stupid to break up with him because no one would put up with me and all of the bad things about me. There was irony to this, as less than a week after leaving him, I met Adam and fell in love with him quickly. Immediately it was obvious we were supposed to be together, but he lived in Arkansas and was only visiting Vegas. So we talked on the phone a lot until our weekend visits, and then I moved in with him two months later.

During my relationship with Rob I found out from his dad that he was actually forty-seven years old while I was twenty-one, but he had lied and said he was thirty-seven. I did not care about his age, only that he lied to me about it. It made me wonder what else he could be hiding from me, though.

I moved in with Adam in March 2008, and in July of that year I got a statement from a credit card that Rob used in the mail. We called it and it was run up to nearly $3,000 in my name. He had done it on three different credit cards, although on two it was a lot less money charged, but it was an ongoing issue for a while. He had started this credit card early in the relationship. Right away I was taken advantage of so he could spend lots of money he didn't have on my credit card, which I was not aware was my card, since I believed it was his, due to his lies.

David Marr

This battle to undo these things was not something I liked putting Adam through, but he was a great help to me at the time. It was eventually stopped with a good cop Adam knew. Rob was not a problem anymore after that, but he sure found a way to mess up as much as he could long after he should have been out of my life. It felt like he destroyed every good memory we could have had, and we had some of those. Now he was just a jerk I shouldn't have spent two seconds of my time with.

Massage School

Massage therapy was something that had appealed to me ever since I'd started giving out foot and shoulder massages in boarding school, and people had told me I was so good at it that I should be a masseuse. One day I got a massage at Massage Envy, and I asked my massage therapist about it. He told me that he only gets pleasant customers that he helps, and they leave happy. There were no crabby customers. This sounded good compared to my casino-bowling desk job I had at the time, where I dealt with rude people constantly. I had thought about and considered massage school, but now it was finally time.

School was challenging, but in a good way, and my teachers were nice. I went to the Nevada School of Massage Therapy in Las Vegas. Unfortunately, I was in a bad class with at least a good portion of my classmates being noisy and misbehaved, but I learned the best I could, and got to keep my books for whenever I wanted to review.

At the beginning I felt that I enjoyed massage, but it was frustrating because we do not know what we are doing yet. My body mechanics kept needing to be improved, I kept needing to be corrected by teachers, etc. It was irritating after a while.

Then the day came, about two months in, when my clinical internship started one day a week on the weekends. To my surprise, I loved it. I loved not being corrected, dealing with it all by myself, correcting myself as I went. It was wonderful. It gave me the boost

I needed to finish school with the confidence that I was doing the right thing.

One day I knew I would be paid for doing it, and it just seemed wonderful. It was a different kind of work because of how much I enjoyed it. In a way it did not feel like work at all. I had an advantage with being able to find knots so automatically and work them out. I found this was not as easy for others as it was for me. It was like having X-ray hands, and clients have always appreciated it.

Sometime later it would be brought to my attention by Adam that this wasn't the only thing with texture that was different to me, and that I would need to try on shirts a lot before buying one because they needed to be soft and feel just right. With Asperger's textures affect me differently, but this ended up working to my advantage in a big way with massage.

I got my Arkansas license in May 2008 and have been using massage ever since.

Meeting Adam

When I met Adam in Vegas less than a week after leaving Rob, I fell for him quickly. Soon it was obvious that we needed to be speaking or spending time together. I was not in a good place with myself at the moment. I had been hurt from Rob and all of the weird and rude stuff he did to make me feel unlovable. I had wished to not be with anyone for at least a year, and then suddenly Adam popped into my life. It was a real curveball. I was not ready for it.

Later I would regret being somewhat of a mess when we met. My life felt crazy at the moment. I went home for two months to spend time with my family, who had been worried sick about the wacky relationship I had been in. For two months Adam and I had a lot of phone time, and weekend visits every couple of weeks. We had a five-day trip in Vegas, which basically felt like the ultimate test to find out if we were going to end up being together or not. We had a wonderful time, and a couple weeks later I was moving to Arkansas.

Being away from him in that time was challenging and just messed me up worse, though. In January of 2008, I moved home to Los Angeles for two months before going to Arkansas, and I felt like I was going insane. I had a staph infection on a toe, and I had to keep soaking it in hot water and iodine. I nearly lost the toe since the infection was terrible, but I obeyed the doctor's orders and it managed to heal. I was still torn up with pain from Rob

(I should have been in counseling but was not) so my head was already messed up.

One day my parents were talking and it became clear to all of us that Mom was getting "stuck on a word" while she was at work. She went to the doctor and we all found out that she had a brain tumor. I felt like I knew right then and there that Mom wasn't going to make it long. We did not know how long she had. Under normal circumstances I would have wanted to stay with my family. I ached to be with Adam, though. I was twenty-two years old, and I needed to make a life for myself.

On one bad night my foot just started gushing blood from out of nowhere and I freaked out and called Dad, who was out at Starbucks with Mom. I didn't know what to do. When Dad came home he got angry and yelled at me and I yelled at him and told him, "Will you stop yelling at me, do you have any idea how hard this is!"

Not nice of me, but I desperately needed him to stop, which he did. Things like that were mounting up, and it was hard for my parents to be compassionate about my near amputation while they were dealing with Mom's brain tumor, and it was an awful thing for the family to have to deal with simultaneously, having to drive me to the hospital for checkups and bandaging all the time. The first visit was a trip to the emergency room where, after someone squeezed all kinds of stuff out of my toe and left the room, I waited on a table for more than a half hour, feeling confused and messed up.

The choice to move in with Adam was not necessarily an easy choice, but it was the right one. I knew that I didn't get along with my overbearing parents enough to get along with them during this difficult time. I don't expect anyone to understand that, but it was what it was, and I visited many times.

Soon I was away from all of that except for my visits, and I had to struggle to figure things out with Adam. I soon found out that I was overly defensive, but only realized it after he pointed it out. He would say something and I'd yell or be hostile back. I was still used to being with someone who would randomly yell at me and my guard was up, so I learned to let my guard down and relax and things went much more smoothly. Sometimes Adam would do something and I would tell him it was just like how Rob did something. The wounds were still too fresh. I had to learn to quit talking about it, but luckily Adam served as a counselor during this time for a while, even though I should have gotten real counseling. It helped us to know each other's backstories, though.

What was also silly was how both our exes were so much alike. Rob would run away when we went out and expect me to run and keep up with him. He refused to just walk, and told me I should just keep up with his crazy fast walking. It turned out Jason, Adam's ex, would do the same to Adam. They were both alike with their rude mannerisms and it was funny to story-swap. At one point, though, Adam nicely asked if I could quit talking about it, and I did. Then an interesting thing happened: I no longer needed to talk about it. It appeared that I was just talking about it out of habit at that point, and it made me keep thinking about it. Suddenly it was all out of me and conversations about him stopped.

Surprise Speech

Later that first year together, my Grandma (on Mom's side), who had been living with my parents, passed away. I did a solo trip to Port Townsend to be with my family and to go to the funeral service for her. I was all hyped up from coffee that trip and had lots of energy. I felt happier than I'd ever been, just newly being with Adam, and was cracking lots of jokes and stuff, and people seemed to enjoy that, and I ended up having an amazing time with everyone.

When it was time for the funeral they invited anyone up to speak if they wanted to speak. My Dad shared something. So did my sister, Erin. I had my hand raised but wasn't being called on yet. I had not planned it, but suddenly realized I had something I wanted to share. Then I got called on.

I went up and shared a story I had not shared with anyone. I talked about how there was one time a few years back where Grandma had put something on the table and I'd gotten scared by her big knuckles with her arthritis in her hands and said something not nice. I explained that if I remembered what it was I would tell them, but I honestly didn't remember. But I knew it was a bad thing to say and someone had told me that it was wrong (it was Philip, but I didn't share that). I felt awful about it and made a point of apologizing to her when we were alone in her kitchen once. I talked with her about it and asked if she forgave me and she smiled and told me that there was nothing to forgive. (I heard an "awww" from a number of audience ladies.) For her it was like it hadn't even happened. I was touched by that, and it showed me how sincere and how kind of a person she was.

I then explained that there were a couple of stories I wanted to share that weren't mine to share, including one with a runaway little kid and a snack bag, and one of her jumping off a rock. Suddenly everyone started laughing and I looked around, confused, wondering what was going on. I wrapped up my little speech and was later informed that the image of an old lady jumping off of a rock was just too silly and made people bust up laughing.

The snack story was of my uncle Steve running away and Grandma and Mom packing him a sack lunch. He ate it in the neighbor's yard and came home and acted like nothing happened. He was little. The jumping-off-the-rock story was of uncle David, and how he would not jump off this giant rock in front of his friends, and how Grandma went up to it and dived off like it was nothing. It was supposed to be funny since his friends were there.

After I spoke about Grandma and we went downstairs to eat and talk about her some more, my sister-in-law, Nicole, my cousin, Justin, my sister, Erin, and at least two other people thanked me for sharing my story. This whole experience meant a lot to me because not long before that I would not have been able to speak in front of people. Just a couple of years earlier I was much more shy about giving speeches, but I had come a long way and was happy about that.

My Dad told me he was proud of me as well when we talked about it, and he later spoke to Adam on the phone and said that I was "like a totally different person" and "a joy to be around" and Adam got to feel special, knowing how much being with him had changed me in those months.

Mom in her younger years.

Mom with me as a baby.

Mom's Sickness

There were many visits to Los Angeles to visit Mom and the family. She got on chemotherapy, which became her life support; she also lost her hair and started wearing a hat. Since the brain tumor was in her left cerebral lobe, it affected her speech and communication. She would mix up pronouns such as "I" or "you," or she might say "he" for "she." For a while she could still play piano despite her difficulty talking, and she had wanted to play for her mother's funeral but was unable to do it. By then it had become too hard for her to play. She took that hard.

We had a final Christmas with all of us, which we all knew would be the last Christmas as a family. One thing I did was give out thirty-dollar Target gift cards to my brothers and Mom and Dad. On Mom's was a picture of girl's shoes. I had weird random ones for my brothers as a joke, like one about a new baby. I walked into the living room a little after and she turned around on the couch and smiled at me.

"Thank you for my — pwesent!" she told me so happily. I hugged her and gave her a kiss on the cheek. It took a lot of effort for her to talk by then, and it was nice to hear.

We had a January visit, and would have had a February visit but an ice storm in Arkansas made that impossible for a while, and then I visited again in March. Mom had been bedridden for a month and the right side of her body would not move and was all bruised up. When she saw me she said "Ohhh ohhh ohhh" and I could see she was happy to see me, though she was glassy eyed, unable to form words. I held her hand while we watched movies like The Long Kiss Goodnight, which was one of her favorites.

For a couple of days, I got to visit with her and keep her company the best that I knew how. At one point I asked if she wanted to be worked on and she said "Yes". I worked on her arms and feet and she said, "Ahh," all relaxed like she was at a spa. She communicated a lot with that even if she couldn't use words. My trip was over though, and it was time to say goodbye to her and so I did, hugs and kisses, and that was that, it was time to go home.

It was three days later that I got a cell-phone message from my Dad letting me know, "Your Mother passed away." I told Adam about it calmly. At first I felt nothing since the shock must not have settled in yet, but the next day it hit me hard and I slept all day and cried over and over. Any time I thought about it I would cry, and it never seemed to end.

In my relationship with Mom, we got along how we got along, with ups and downs. Sometimes there was a lot of arguing, but we worked things out in the ways that we did. We also had a lot of nice conversations too, and we talked more about being gay and things like that than I did with any other family member. Losing Mom was losing the one family member who came the closest to understanding me and the complexities of Asperger's. I lost the one person who had the best chance of ever understanding me, of being able to explain things about me in a matter-of-fact way that no one else could.

There were times when Mom had come to my defense to explain something about me that she knew, but I didn't even understand about myself. She explained how I had preliminaries before saying something, even if it wasn't necessary, such as saying I didn't want to be harsh with something. She also once mentioned how I was someone who said things as they were and didn't beat around the bush. I was surprised at that. I didn't even realize I did that when she said it.

Sometimes my Asperger's could be my own worst enemy, and if it wanted to punish me, then it would punish me. Much more than what is fair. It even might have seemed downright psychotic. My naturally obsessive nature took a wild-beast nature of its own, and every bad thing I had ever said to Mom, every argument, stuff from more than ten years ago, kept coming back to look me in the eye and guilt me — bad memories swirling through my mind over and over and over and I would want them to stop, but they would not.

Pretty soon I spent $1,500 on counseling in only two months. My brain just didn't feel functional. Bad memories from tenth grade were swirling around all the time. It was the worst year of my life, and I thought it was all behind me. When we are teenagers, though, our brain is supposed to be reorganizing, and maybe some of it just wasn't put away properly. I had to go through so much all over again, which I never expected.

My brothers cried a lot too, though I was not around to see it, and my Dad remarried in five months, which did not surprise me in the slightest. Adam and I had talked about it, and I always remembered, growing up, if someone called for Dad we were not to give it to him, because, in Dad's own words, he had no friends and it was always a salesperson. It was known that Mom was Dad's one friend and that's the kind of man he was — either that or working long hours at his lawyer office. I've asked him probably at least ten times what he did for a living but never understood it. He was a lawyer, and that was enough.

That year we had a funeral for my Mother, a cousin's wedding, my Dad's wedding, my brother Stephen's wedding, and my brother

Philip's wedding. We all moved on the best we could, in the ways we knew how. The following February, Nicole and Philip had their first baby together. Stella Leslie Marr was named after, and would also have the same initials, as her grandmother, Sarah Leslie Marr.

Struggling with Adam

Some things in my relationship with Adam I continued to struggle with. I was not disciplined enough about cleaning the house, and I knew as much. Part of it was that I was not good at organizing. Some stuff I wasn't sure where I could even put it. Yes, I can throw everything in a big box, but shouldn't I try to do better than that? Even if it's slow? Papers bugged me; I would have to look over each one carefully before throwing one away. Sometimes I wrote a phone number that was important on one.

It has been said about Aspies that we are freakishly organized in certain ways, but in other ways we are not at all. This definitely applied to me. Some things, like scheduling, homework, organizing video games alphabetically, I cared about. Some stuff I did not, or was not sure of a better way to do it.

Growing up as the third of five kids, though, I was used to our pretty decently sized, some would say large, three-story house being trashed all the time, with guests constantly coming in and out. The house was always a mess, no matter what we did, and if it was clean it was not for long. I was used to that. As I've said many times, "I have to remind myself that it is messy." It may seem normal when we are used to that growing up. We may have to remind ourselves that we want to be better than that. First throw away trash, then organize things better, get a rhythm going so things don't look like a trash can.

There were a lot of things Adam didn't "get" about me at first and a huge one was the house clean-up problem, but there were other things too. I would (unintentionally) blame him for stuff due to a defensive nature I had. I needed to learn to quit doing that.

Sometimes our words can be clumsy with Asperger's, though; we don't always know when something comes across as rude. We may have meant for something to be taken completely differently, we may have to say it over again and apologize later. I also grew up with a family that was constantly getting mad, shifting the blame all the time, so I thought this was normal, to never apologize and to blame the other person instead of accepting responsibility. After all, growing up I saw Mom and Dad do it all the time, so wasn't this how we were supposed to talk?

Being in a long-term committed relationship, it becomes obvious quickly that if all we do is shift blame, we are going to have a bad time. Apologies are crucial, and so is admitting exactly what you did wrong so you can be better. Cement the relationship with hope; let the other person know what you will work on and exactly what you plan to do.

Don't wait until things are dark and bad until getting a couples counseling session. By then the sessions will be frustrating, with too many negative things to cover, and it will always feel like we need more time. Even good relationships, I think, would benefit from one couples counseling session a month, and getting some honest feedback and perspective within the relationship. This is especially important if one has Asperger's, because there will always be something, at least something small, to figure out, such as time management, or assigning duties with the house.

The couples counseling sessions did not feel like they were helping. It may have been partly incompatibility with the counselor, or that our relationship was too far gone by then, or that one or both of us were too angry and fed up to make the relationship work, but over time it became more and more apparent that we needed to split up. Adam's understanding of Asperger's, his understanding of me, felt limited. When two people are fighting and angry constantly and they don't even understand each other clearly in the first place, it is hard, if not impossible, for them to get onto solid ground.

For instance, there were the times he got mad at me because I "looked angry" in restaurants due to stimulus overload. I didn't mean to look like that, and would try to relax, but it wouldn't work. I didn't like loud restaurants and faking it felt impossible, although I did get better at smiling politely over time. My super-fast compulsive eating, in time, became better too, with more minor slip-ups here and there, but I know it was bad at the beginning of our relationship.

One day I had to call my Dad and explain to him I was going to need to be picked up at an airport. I had a surprisingly nice talk with Adam on the way there. We closed a lot of conversations and had many important things answered. In a way it was hard to leave with that, but in a way we sort of made peace with what had to happen. Los Angeles wasn't my favorite place, but I could have a roof over my head until I figured out my next move.

Separation

During the time we were separated we continued to talk on the phone; we even had weekend visits a few times. I was not sure what Adam and I were, or what to call it. Family members were surprised and supportive that I was continuing to be in contact with him. My family loved Adam. I always felt that he was a "people person" that way.

We went to A'Float Sushi, which had boats of sushi going around the water to grab. That was and continues to be our favorite restaurant in the area, and it's in Pasadena.

We were having a nice conversation, and I remember getting to a point where I started saying, "I may not be bringing home the most money but I gave you hugs and kisses, and made you feel loved and—"

"Stop."

I looked over at Adam and saw he was teary-eyed.

"I'm sorry! I'm sorry. I'll change the subject okay?" I said while rubbing his back a bit. I felt like the biggest jerk in the world. I did not mean to make him feel bad, but it also showed me how much he loved me.

There were a lot of things we needed to sort out over six months. It was complicated. People did not know what was going on or why we were still in contact. There were some arguments, some good times, and at the time Adam did not understand Asperger's the way he needed to in order for the relationship to continue.

We had a big argument once, which partly included the fact that he was mad that I could not take a hint in a conversation where he was attempting to change the subject because he did not want to talk about something. I did not get it. I got frustrated with that and yelled at him that this was something that he needed to understand two years ago. That was one of the first things I explained about myself to him back when we first met, and still he did not get it. In every Asperger book we ever read, trying to change the subject is a "nonverbal social cue" and every author specifically warned not to do it. This was not new information. Adam did not see how to apply it. There was a large disconnect with applying the information.

He read the book *House Rules* by Jodi Picoult and it opened his eyes to all that he did not understand. There was a part in the book about how the mom did not want her son to drive; Adam heard this on audiobook and needed to pull over and cry for a while. He knew all about my story with my Mom not letting me drive, and this hit him hard. A lot of things in the book showed him what he needed to know, and what he lacked understanding about.

Ultimately, at the end of our six months apart, my staying in LA came to an end when Adam and I were ready for me to move home. There was a massage job that I wanted and I had a strong feeling I would get if I applied. They needed people and it was kind of in the middle of nowhere and they were "always hiring." I wanted to apply, but it was clear to Adam and me that we should move in together again. We have lived together ever since, and understanding between us has always been improving.

YouTube

The world seemed to change when I got back to Arkansas in a big way. Gay suicides were starting to become national news and made big waves. I remembered how suicidal I'd felt when I was fifteen and felt impacted. I felt obligated to speak up.

I shared my coming out story on YouTube, which was well-received, but since then I have felt that was too personal and put it on private, but for a long time it was not and it led to a number of other videos. People asked me questions, and I would have a video to answer it. This happened over and over.

My original plan was to make only a couple of videos to address gay issues. That way, it was unlikely anyone in my area would find the videos. Boy did it not work out that way. Pretty soon I had a hundred videos up, and I did not want to take them down. I had to accept my fate that pretty soon people were going to see them.

Not everyone understands how YouTube works. Neither did I at first. I made the stupid mistake of listing my primary email address rather than a throwaway, which ended up leading people on my email contact list to it. I had marked something in the settings saying people who had my email address would not know about the YouTube videos, which I guess did not work. It made no difference. Everyone I knew found it anyway, and eventually people in my area as well.

I had to decide what to put on private and what to keep up; stuff that I did not care was public suddenly became a bigger issue, but I got used to it and got over it the best I could.

What I had not anticipated was how mentioning that I had Asperger's in the coming-out video would lead to people asking me more questions about that. Pretty soon I saw there was a need for videos about Asperger's, as well. In fact, there was a much bigger need for those than for the gay-themed video monologues. Far more people were already making those.

People were extremely supportive. Since I kept changing themes for the videos back and forth, one day I decided to make a public playlist of the Asperger videos and see if that would do anything. Right away I got a couple messages from people thanking me for my Asperger videos. Putting the videos in a public playlist made a huge difference. People could locate and watch them all much more easily.

Not only was making videos helping other people understand the various nuances of Asperger's, but it was helping me understand things better as well. Sometimes something in a comment would lead to me making a video in response, or enhance my understanding with certain odd things about it.

I saw that people with Asperger's were asking questions an unusual amount, so I made a video explaining issues I'd used to have with asking questions too much. I saw someone with Asperger's was saying "I love you like a brother, (if that's okay)." It reminded me how I used to double-check odd things as an OCD. One helpful thing was when I saw that a man with Asperger's would correct things I would say, and tell me how I should have said something else instead. This was something Adam had specifically asked me to stop doing, so that hit hard.

Asperger's: A Literal Journey

I have explained to people before that this is a potential issue with people with Asperger's. They do not see it as correcting. This is their way of processing what you have said. After Adam asked me to quit doing that, and after seeing someone else doing it and seeing it as pretty obnoxious, it gave me the confirmation I needed to quit doing it.

In one video I mentioned how noisy restaurants were bad for me, and how it just made me look like I was angry. I did not mean to do it, but it was something that happened. Since then I have become better at staying more relaxed and smiling, though. I keep a better attitude and face, just like Mom always wanted me to do, but I had previously felt unable to do.

The more I made videos and the more I spoke with people the more I learned. What I learned greatly facilitated what I still needed to learn, and include in a book, which has been a work in progress in my thoughts and notes for some time now. The ideas within it were constantly evolving regarding what was necessary to talk about. My over-analytical nature made it tough sometimes, but it was important to just keep writing, re-writing, and edit it to flow better.

I was grateful that I'd started making videos and it did change my life in a big way. I hope that family members understood that talking about certain things was for the greater good, and I did what I could to not include names and keep things a little vague. My older brother Philip indicated once that he'd seen them when he hinted that I should take down the videos of his family. I honestly forgot those were there. They were only there as a way of backing them up before I did much with that channel. I respected his wishes and put those on private. That was the one and only time any family member has spoken with me about the channel, apart from my sister Erin, with whom I have a more open way of sharing than I do with my Dad and three brothers.

I had made my username long before the suicides, kind of as a joke, not realizing it would get far or that I would be making any serious content on it. At the time I had recently found out California had started to ban gay marriage. We had gotten a license to get married there before that, being told no matter what it would be good for a couple months. It was banned anyway and our license was suddenly good for nothing, which nobody who helped us obtain the license had expected. As my gay revenge, to rub my gayness in everyone's face, SillyGayBoy was born.

Walmart

Coming back home to Arkansas, I still worked for myself by doing massage at home. Work was slow and that was unfortunate; it had not always been slow. I was making good money when I first started doing it. That was when the recession happened and suddenly people did not have money for massages anymore. I kept looking for jobs, but did not have any luck. I also had a computer addiction for a while where it was hard for me to get off the computer sometimes. I do believe that I am better socially because of my time on a computer, though I am not sure this is always the case with people, but with Asperger's, I feel that it has helped me continue developing socially.

I had to learn to break myself away from a computer and job hunt more, and when I did I had no success for quite a while. I went through around twenty to fifty applications before I finally got to Walmart. Something I did not take into account that I should have was that I should have been applying at places that had more jobs available. Walmart is one of those types of places. I went in with open availability, and made sure to smile and be nice to a manager and told her that my intention was to have a job and do massage around the job, just so I was clear on that, because currently doing massages was in my application. I guess it worked, too, because soon I was called for an interview, and then a drug test, and I would start a maintenance job a day or so after.

I'd never considered doing janitorial work, which they call "maintenance." That is actually more descriptive. We maintain clean areas. I needed a job too badly to turn it down, no matter how I felt about it, and felt that I would just get another job within Walmart when the time came. They like that to be six months in.

It turned out I liked the job too much to even want another job. I was not sure what to expect, but to my surprise I loved it. People left me alone, I worked pretty independently with a couple of other people, and I had my own things to be in charge of, like gloves and all the cleaning supplies. I found nearly everything clicked with me about the job.

When I kept busy for a full shift, time just flew by. I always had tons of stuff to do with little tasks. I found that taking Adderall helped, too. When I was not taking it I found that it made me panic thinking of what thing I would do next, while when I took Adderall I would think that I would do this one thing, then this, then this, and it organized it in a list, and showed me what the bigger priorities were.

I kept at the job, with a good pace, and I felt respected for doing so. I even was commended for doing things that other workers had continued to avoid. It felt good, and people knew they could come to me if they needed help.

The one thing it did not do so much good for was my body. My joints and muscles in my lower and mid back acted up. The work and what it did to those areas did not agree with me at all. But since then I've learned tons of little tricks to help things be better. At some point though, the job needed to end, no matter how much I liked it, due to those body issues.

My temper got the best of me sometimes. I was doing the ladies bathroom once and I heard several women outside complaining about how long it would take and how it would take forever, while I was busting my butt to get it done as fast as possible. These types of ladies were a continuous problem, as everyone feels they deserve to come in and make me wait instead of going to the other bathroom. Anyway, these ladies were talking and I lost it and marched over to them and said, "WE DON'T ALLOW CUSTOMERS TO STAND OUTSIDE AND COMPLAIN THE WHOLE TIME SOMEONE'S TRYING TO CLEAN!! PLEASE GO WAY FAR AWAY, SOMEPLACE ELSE!!!!"

I could have gotten in trouble for that, but luckily I did not. In fact, the CSM (Customer Service Manager) station was only a few feet away. But I was lucky and the ladies just went away. I needed to watch it, and be more careful, but little things set me off sometimes. But mostly, I feel I was nice to people.

I was talking to one manager once about joining the produce section. He caught me once at a bad moment where I had forgotten to take my Adderall and walked a little slower than normal with my cleaning cart, daydreaming just a little. He took me aside and explained to me, "Managers look for people who can stay on a task with a good pace, just letting you know."

I told him that I was scared of hitting someone with the cart, but that I would go faster.

Anyway, I took his advice and ended up finding a good pace. I had some entries in for different jobs that I would be willing to take, and IMS (Inventory Management System) was one. The manager Ted was looking for people to hire for that, and my name popped up. He had always greeted me when I passed him, and one day the time came when he needed someone to fill a job. He liked my brisk way of working, and thought if I could apply that there it would be a great fit.

I had already had to help the second-shift IMS, and it was not a good fit at all. I even explained that to him. He wanted me to try anyway since our first shift would be totally different than the second shift. He knew the numbers were hard for me, remembering all those numbers and codes, but he wanted me anyway.

Getting out of maintenance was important even if it was in a roundabout way. It is okay to try something new and it might not be for everyone. It should be okay anyway, but it was not here. People were terrible, particularly my trainer, Rachel. Everyone seemed to just assume that I would learn things just as fast as they did. It did not work that way. The numbers for the item locations were awfully hard for me to learn.

It was tough having a trainer like Rachel, who basically yelled at me anytime I needed to ask a question. I needed to have another trainer but it did not seem like an option. One day I had the opportunity to work five weeks at night doing a different project. I took it and enjoyed it. I had always wanted to work at night to see what it was like, and some of the night crew were my favorite associates there. It was simpler work, and I was better at it.

When it was over and I went back to working days again, my issues with Rachel were right where I'd left them. There had already been a point where two associates, including Rachel, were asked to be more patient with me. Then one day a worker came up to me and said, "I don't care what she says, I think you're a great worker." By "she" he meant Rachel, who was talking trash about me where I couldn't hear it. I finally lost it and blew up.

"IF YOU ARE BEING SERIOUS RIGHT NOW SHE IS REALLY NOT SUPPOSED TO BE DOING THAT!!!"

The guy ran away scared (I apologized to him later; he was fine with me). I passed by Rachel a minute later and she looked scared of me. Guilty. She totally did it. Not only was she an awful woman anytime I needed to learn anything, but she was talking about me behind my back as well. She was supposed to be my trainer. I was furious the rest of the day. I have blood pressure problems, and my blood pressure skyrocketed for the remainder of the day, even hours after I'd come home.

I told Ted about it the following day as soon as I came in, and two managers had a talk with her. My overall impression was that this was a talk that was a long time coming and she was self-conscious about hearing it. It seemed like she was crying since she suddenly ran away, then later would not be around me and just acted like I was not around when she had to work near me.

One of the things I asked Ted when we had our talk was if there was any way I could work in the other area without Rachel. He said that this was not a possibility as that area was more difficult. I felt I was out of options and volunteered to step down. The job was not working, and I did not want to work around Rachel another second anyway.

Unfortunately, people were on her side and things got weird with the other associates. A male associate, Jesse, became extremely rude suddenly; and it was obvious it was to get back at me. Nobody knew how to be neutral with the situation and a lot of people just wanted to make excuses for her, although I know I was not the only person to have problems with her. Even Adam saw that she was yelling at another employee about something when he went to Walmart once. She even did it in front of customers.

My time doing IMS came to a close and soon I became a cart associate/stock associate and had to go to the back with a six-wheeler, getting TVs from those same people. I did my best to put on a polite face, although they acted odd around me. My feeling was that a couple of them felt bad that they had been as mean as they were, and that I had left. I was fine with leaving (my hurt from the experiences there, not so much, but that would go away in time). I just wish people were more open about how not everyone learns the same, but they didn't want to be. Now I had a different position and it was no longer my problem.

Being a cart associate seemed like a simple enough job, that I did not feel like I could mess up. Not only that, but I liked the physical work part of it. That agrees with some people. Being outside, shoving things around, getting in shape; it seemed like fun stuff to me. And it was! I enjoyed it. That job clicked with me the most out of all three.

Going to the carry-outs to help with customers was nice too. I got my people time as well! Working with IMS, I was always looking at boxes and my social skills suffered. Making eye contact became difficult and it became harder to socialize. Switching to being a cart associate changed that, in a big way, and socializing became part of the job again and it helped me a lot, just like I'd enjoyed taking orders at In-N-Out Burger. These were parts of the job I liked that helped me.

There was sort of a back and forth with certain associates where they kept trying to get away with hiding for long periods of time, even as much as three hours, and other things. I did not want to fight about everything, but there were times I needed to be able to do my job and there was no other way to do it than to tell a manager something. It was a difficult situation to be in, and it was ongoing.

Ross had a couple times yelled at me for being on "his side" and this was becoming problematic. One day I was closing and could not be on "his side," according to him, and by the time I could there was no way to put all the carts away on time. This was a problem. It was interfering with my work and he was standing in my way, which could get me in trouble.

I came to Jodi in the office and asked if there was a time I could speak with him. He told me I could speak with him now. I said, "Okay…say I am closing one night. Would it be okay if from time to time I want to check both sides and make sure that everything is getting wrapped up okay?"

Jodi seemed more surprised than I expected.

"Absolutely, you guys are supposed to be a team."

"…Okay, Ross isn't letting me do that. And I have tried to work this out on my own, Jodi, he will not listen to me, he will *not*, he yells over me until he gets his way. Whatever his reasons are for claiming it is 'his side' I don't care, he may be trying to get away with stuff, but that is not important to me right now, but I do need to be able to do my work and he is standing in my way."

Jodi immediately spoke with Ross and it got cleared up. I appreciated Jodi for that and he took it seriously. But things were never that simple. At some point Ross was going to want to do some dumb revenge move like they always wanted to do.

It was near the end of my time as a cart associate that our cat Delilah basically aged really fast. It seemed she became blind, walked funny, waited for people to put her down instead of jumping to the ground; everything seemed bad. It hit me and Adam hard. We loved our one cat. I hated seeing her struggle like that, but she was twenty-six years old in human years, and she had a long life. One day it came time to put her down. She had water in her lungs, and her breathing became difficult. That is not a good way to go, so we did it as peacefully and humanely as possible. I talked to her, stroked her, and Adam and I were in the room. We were shattered. It was hard to say goodbye to her. There was a lot of crying that day.

I came in with my wounds from Delilah being put down the day before fresh. If anyone had asked me if I was okay to go to work, I would 100% have told them that I was. Nothing even felt wrong. I felt fine. I started the day just like any other.

I was on the grocery side, which was our busier side. Tommy and Ross were on the GM side (general merchandise), which was our less busy side. They walked together while they worked, enjoying their time together. No, we are not supposed to do that, but I don't care, normally. But this was a Saturday that was unusually busy.

I busted my butt to try to keep the carts in the bay. In no time they were all taken. The cart associates were called for carry-outs. I should have said the bay was too low but did not; I did the carry-outs anyway, since the others were ignoring the radio calls. I called on the radio to see if someone could help. Ross said he would come later. An hour later I called to talk to Tommy. Ross answered and said that Tommy was busy, and just went out of his way to be obnoxious and talk for him.

A panic attack was starting; I felt like it was different this time, like I was starting to have a heart attack. I felt my insides shaking, I felt tears starting to come and burn my eyes. I knew what these episodes were like, although I had not had one in years. If anyone saw me having a crying meltdown, it would scare the heck out of them. This was not an option.

I went to the back, slid my card; I was clocking out.

I went over to a CSM and, trying to hold back tears, explained to her that I could not do this on my own and that I'd already called them twice on the radio and they had no intention of helping. I was sorry, but there was nothing more that I could do. I had to go home.

I left. I went to Petco instead of home. I visited a cat, Chester, who we had seen a few days before. I already had a name for him, but Adam said we were not getting any more animals. I was having an awful day and I needed to visit him again, for the last time. He would be able to comfort me.

I asked a woman about him and found out he was already adopted. I mentioned something about our cat Delilah, and the woman said that the person adopting him also had a cat named Delilah.

Oops. Adam had meant to surprise me. I totally spoiled the surprise.

I texted Adam about it. He was not happy, but I did not want a lying relationship with him. He had meant for the cat to randomly walk into the house. He wanted to see the happy look on my face. I took that away through unforeseen events.

I went to bed that night so happy. Before I could go to bed I went back to Chester over and over to pet him and talk to him. I loved my Chester so much. He was four years old, and a Russian Blue. He was the biggest-boned cat I had ever seen. I just loved him. I was nuts about him, and had a huge connection with him that I did not usually have with animals. He would crawl all over my chest, lick me right in the face; he was fantastic.

I got a call from Jodi that I somehow missed, and he left a voicemail. I called back and talked to a different manager, Christina, who was willing to hold my job for a day, and asked me to please never do that again. She told me Jodi went right out and talked to Tommy and Ross and was not happy about it. Christina was shocked that I'd called over the radio twice, and was not happy about that part at all. She told me the CSMs should have heard it and done something about it, but they were probably focusing on the cashiers.

I went back to work. Some people seemed shocked to see me. My immediate coworkers just seemed sympathetic. Billy wanted to know what happened. I told him I didn't want to talk about it. Managers knew what happened (except for the full details of the meltdown which I didn't think they would understand). Everyone else could assume whatever they wanted. I was through spelling it out for people.

I had always been interested in acting, but with Walmart it did not seem possible. My schedule was all over the place, and I left it that way on purpose. I wanted to have open availability and a lot of hours. I did, however, get to be in a short film called Haunted as a ghost once, which was fun. It was the only thing I got to do while working at Walmart for acting.

Pretty soon *Shadow Bound* was going to be filmed. It was going to be a five-episode black-and-white horror web series that would later be edited into a movie. I knew I had to get in this one. I sent in a video audition. Later I was given a part with a two-episode story arc. My part would be in episodes four and five.

I made it extremely clear to Jodi that there were two days where there was a 0% chance of me coming to work, and that I would be in Springfield for filming. This was two weeks before filming. Unfortunately, this was also a busy week, possibly a sale week, and nothing was checked into by management. A week before filming, I checked again and there was no way to get any shifts switched with mine.

Adam was starting his new massage business, where I could do massage full time. The time was coming to switch to that anyway.

Walmart could no longer accommodate my schedule, and my different schedules could not merge any further.

I wrote a note explaining the two days that I would not be able to work, saying, "I have already been speaking with management about this and we have already tried, but we are unable to get these shifts switched with anyone. Therefore, Saturday August 21st has to be my final day. Best wishes, David Marr." I regretted a little not thanking them for hiring me, but I did not think of it in time.

I needed them to know why it needed to be then. People were decent to me about it. A couple people even looked extremely sad and disappointed that I was leaving. I basically left out the back door, metaphorically, before most people even knew I was leaving. I would bump into people later that had no idea why I left. I guess I should have told more people.

Walmart gave me tons of hours with my open availability. I worked around 10 months in Maintenance, three months in I.M.S. and one year and two months as a cart associate, for an estimated two years and two months. In that time, I also finished my Bachelor's in Psychology online. But now, my world opened up to the world of acting.

Headshot.

My look for Shadow Bound.

Acting

In most ways I felt *Shadow Bound* was sort of like an awakening into acting. I did get to be a ghost in the short film *Haunted* for the short-film festival Sato, and even got an IMDb credit, but *Shadow Bound* in most ways felt like the first thing. There was so much to learn every day on set; I took it all in and was so happy for all that I could learn and absorb.

One day we got an email the day of that told us important information. I did not have a lot of time since I needed to shower, get ready to leave, pack, leave, and then drive two and a half hours to our destination, but both Adam and I believed the email was switching the time to 2:30 instead of 2:00. I believed I was showing up fifteen minutes early but actually showed up fifteen minutes late. I did not realize it until later on, and I felt terrible about it. Even though they weren't ready to shoot for another forty-five minutes, it still looked bad and I tore myself apart over it.

I beat myself up over it for three days straight and spoke to my counselor about it. Tracy told me I needed to consider getting on an anti-anxiety medication. I did go to the doctor and got it and started using it as needed, and found that it helped. I no longer had the constant need to beat myself up nonstop over something, or think in circles like that anymore. I could not take it past a certain time or I would risk getting sleepy, but it helped a lot.

Appearances were important with acting. I was told by the creator, Nathan, to read the script for the fifth episode, which I guess did not mean right then, but I went ahead and took it that way anyway. Since my printer was not working at my house I had to read it from my phone, and that, coupled with being late, got me a dirty, annoyed look from someone when we were about to film. I was doing what Nathan asked me to do, but it made no difference. I looked like I was playing with my phone, and that was bad.

From then on I made a point of having two scripts for every shoot, since there was always someone who did not have one, and it needed to be printed and in binders. It is also better for two or more people to see it at the same time if necessary.

As for showing up and not having a lot of time before the shoot and understanding things incorrectly, I decided that if the shoot was early enough in the day I would just be spending the night before in Springfield, Missouri at a hotel. I learned I needed to show up early and relax with shooting. It is not uncommon for me to be an hour or more early. I liked the time to study the script and talk to people who were hanging around; it made going into filming nice that way.

I was asked to be a Hollow One for the final day of shooting, which required us to wear these tight white tights. We had make-up that covered our front but was not necessary for the back this time. I was afraid of putting on more clothes and messing up the makeup, so I didn't. This was stupid because it was freezing cold, but I expected us to be filmed quickly — but we weren't. At one point I left a group of people to hear a girl say, "Yeah, it's weird," and I knew she was talking about me. Nathan kind of hinted to me to put clothes on as well, and I started to put some hints together. I did not mean to make anyone uncomfortable, just wanted to be ready for shooting and not mess up my makeup. My bad.

There are people who can draw, and I can't, so I need acting to be my art. I learned a lot through *Shadow Bound*. I learned that as a naturally intense person, I gravitated towards intense roles. Not only that, but people would start wanting me for that with different kinds of projects. I also would go out of my way to pursue those kinds of roles, and sometimes with great success, too. I never took a rejection personally. I either fit into a film project or I don't. But with *Shadow Bound* came better success to follow, and some demo-reel footage that would show what I could bring to an intense role.

I found that there were even people who, upon seeing the demo reel, would immediately want to work with me and offer a role. It made the difference between having nothing and having a role sometimes.

I also learned some tricks about learning my lines, both from experience and from an acting class I took with George Cron, in Springfield, Missouri. Not only was it helpful to read a script with pink highlighting, but it also helped to say my lines into a tape recorder of some sort (I use an iPhone app), and record things in different ways and play them with headphones while I was walking around the house doing chores. I would sometimes perform them, say them along with it, or just listen, but it always helped. I found that recording audio worked far better than I thought it would, and seemed to be a neat trick to learn the lines fast. It got to where I could remember lines automatically, although initially it is always a struggle to learn and I need to have patience.

I auditioned for *Penny Man*, which was a story about a schizophrenic time traveler. I wanted to audition for "Victor", but they said it was taken, so instead, I auditioned to be a voice in a character's head, titled "Male." I immediately loved all his lines and looked forward to the voice acting. We had certain issues with production delays, and at some point when we were going to start filming, the actor for "Victor" dropped out and I was asked to be

"Victor" instead. It turned out I got to be him anyway, and it was a bigger and better role.

Victor had weird OCD tics and rocked back and forth, and was rapidly analytical about everything. It seemed like a fun twist of fate that I was asked to play this part instead, as this man had a degree of Autism, while I had a higher-functioning kind, which, as far as I knew, nobody even knew. I'd had a lot of these traits in the past, even currently, and all I had to do was exaggerate them. I felt that I knew how, and was told I did it well.

I have been in a number of things, some smaller and some larger. Moving to Arkansas with Adam, there were certain things I needed to let go of, but one thing I always look forward to is acting, which has always been fun and nice. I always had the patience to go through takes lots of times in different ways, just like I do when I am practicing lines on my own.

It helps to understand everything possible in the script in advance, and I go through it tons of times in my head in different ways, although this is not always possible. Sometimes with filming there is a lot that is made up on the spot, and we just have to go along with it the best we can.

It was nice that I would have a hobby to look forward to, and it felt good. I was never interested in plays. I was only interested in film, and enjoyed the concept of doing things over and over again in different ways. I felt a stronger sense of what the "acting bug" was. With *Shadow Bound* I had such an amazing experience with episodes four and five. I could not get enough of it. Although the other acting experiences were incredibly different, and did not have tons of makeup and horror props and masks, I still enjoyed it every time.

Karaoke

There are different things I have tried out for fun over the years, and at some point I landed on Karaoke. I loved singing, I found that Karaoke bars had a lot of songs that I liked, not all of them, but plenty to choose from. I went to gay and straight bars but mostly a gay one I liked.

I gave it a try and at first I was awful. It was weird and unsettling. The sound was much different than I had anticipated. It came from one speaker, far away, and I felt like I couldn't hear myself, and I wasn't sure what I was doing.

I kept at it though and the second time I was better, by the third time I felt like I knew what I was doing. It got more fun the more I did it. It helped to have a couple drinks first and then I didn't care if it turned out embarrassing or not.

I got better with some practice and pretty soon I made friends with a couple people I ended up having a lot of adventures with, and they introduced me to other people. That is the thing about music, it brings people together, and it gives people something to talk about.

One day I picked the song "Lips of an Angel" by Hinder. I missed that song. I noticed when I thought to myself "this is easy" when I picked a song it seemed to always turn out better.

I picked the song and turned in my slip of paper and it was my turn to sing on a packed night. I sang it. I loved it. I wasn't paying attention to the other people. The song wrapped up. The audience roared with applause and I freaked out and ran to my seat with my friend and sat down. I wasn't ready for that and was not expecting that at all. Responses had started to be more positive.

After my improvement with the public response I sang "Disease" by Matchbox Twenty and had a similar loud response. I had begun to get used to it.

On one visit I had a terrible day and some awful things had happened. I was in a real funk and tried to fake happy because I was being introduced to a friend of my friend. I wondered if music could make me feel better like it always seemed to.

I picked "Out of My Heart (Into Your Head)" by BBMak. One noteworthy thing about the song was that there is a long climax at one part. I went ahead and sang the song, on a night more packed then any night I had been there.

I see the crowd and everyone is talking, minding their business. We had regulars that always picked the same song each week and people seemed to have tuned them out.

The song began. "I feel fine" I sang. Everyone looked at me all at once. What was that about? I guess they liked my voice.

I continued singing and enjoying it. I reached the climax of the song. Something strange happened that never happened before. The energy in the room got bigger and bigger and it felt like it was waiting to explode. The last word of this part stretches out quite a bit:

> *Take a look at the sky*
> *Feel the sunshine*
> *In your heart*
> *In your head*
> *In your own time*

Asperger's: A Literal Journey

People actually cheered, *loud*, mid-song! That had never happened before! I finished the song to loud applause. My bad day had elated. It all washed away. I was happy again.

Some random guy came up to me and said: "You're cute and you can sing!"

If someone is on the Autism spectrum and they feel they can hit notes well with singing, give karaoke a try. You might be surprised what happens.

Wallyball

Sometimes I think back on when I could not catch a big rubber ball until the special day in 5th grade where I was finally able to. In my early years certain things with coordination did not come easy. Some years down the road as an adult, things were quite different. I had tried out many things. Some things I even seemed to have some skill at.

One thing I loved doing was at one gym we had Wallyball, which is basically like Volleyball but in a Racquetball court. I always enjoyed and had some skill with Volleyball and this sport just came easier than many others.

At Walmart working as a cart associate my schedule was all over the place, but I showed up when I was able to. I found that when I walked in the people seemed to rejoice when I arrived. Why? I didn't talk all that much. I was pretty quiet, I just came there to play. It seemed that people got excited because when I arrived it shook the game up quite a bit from their usual play.

I loved it. It was always the highlight of my week. I found there were loads of times where the other side would start talking to each other because there were shots that just looked impossible to get, yet I would be fast enough to get it, and would quickly score a point off of them.

I guess I was pretty memorable, since many of them would talk to me later when they saw me, even if I had only met them a couple of times and could not remember meeting them. They always seemed so positive when they talked to me. It would seem as if I left an impression.

One day working at Walmart I randomly saw a guy who had been there a couple times. He quickly chatted with me and reminisced with me about how when he had played people on his side were getting angry and aggravated because I had kept scoring too many points on them, and it was causing a lot of frustration. He was telling me about this with a smile. I guess he thought it was funny.

Back in 5th grade I may not have ever believed I would ever be good at something, but my advice to Asperger kids and their parents is to try as many sports as possible. There may be things they might unexpectedly be quite good at.

For me Volleyball, Wallyball, and Dodgeball seemed among those things. Some of us just have natural reflexes that make those things a lot easier, but it takes trying new things to find out what works for us.

"Good With Kids"

There have been different situations throughout life where I had been told I was "good with kids". In my church I grew up in, there was a time once a week where single moms could come and be fed, and people could play games and things with the kids. It was a great time once a week and I was told I was their "main man, if you aren't there kids are asking where you are."

Over time I also enjoyed doing other things like babysitting or volunteering with kids in different ways. Reading stories, helping them learn to read, those things were a lot of fun and satisfying.

What I found was a lot of adults and parents got frustrated with things I didn't think were a huge deal. I just felt more mellow around them. I talked to them as if they were my friend and not down to them as if they were a kid. We had fun. I played video games with them and sometimes had to beat levels for them.

I just think with Asperger's things came differently to me. I knew I was literal. I knew I wanted people to be straight forward with me and not everyone would be. I knew what I needed as a kid and what people were unable and unwilling to do, and how communication could just seem needlessly complicated.

I knew how to talk to kids, how to be patient, and how to be straight forward with them when they had questions. A lot of things just came naturally for me that did not come naturally to a lot of grownups I saw.

It was nice having kids like me. It is said about Asperger's that we may like to talk to people that are a lot older or a lot younger.

That definitely seemed true for me, at least sometimes. I enjoyed hanging out with kids just like I enjoyed talking to teachers at school, sometimes more than people my age. People my age sometimes just seemed boring.

With things to do for work, one thing I had turned down as an option was something like being a court reporter. At a young age I could type 72 words a minute and probably more and more if I had kept testing it. Yet this didn't seem like an option. I have bad A.D.D., I don't like to sit still, so sitting for an 8-hour shift typing just seemed out of the question, even if I could make a lot of money off of it. It wasn't something I felt like I could do. I need to move around more than that with my jobs.

However, things with kids always seemed like an option and one I felt I could possibly return to at some point. It was something I enjoyed and felt like I was good at. I guess the only thing that kept me from those options with career goals was that I enjoyed doing massage for work so much, I never wanted to do anything else. It just worked so much as a job. It never felt like work. I always felt I would enjoy something else less.

But working with kids was always an option and always one that had been considered.

Coping with Asperger's

Throughout my years with Adam there have been many tics that I started with that eventually I learned coping skills to stop. Relationships are so helpful to people with Asperger's. If they care to be in them, and to be with someone who is good for them, then there is an infinite amount of personal growth. I am grateful to have had that, and it accelerated my personal growth so much more than just being alone or socializing as a single man.

Dishes were hard for me at the beginning. I don't know why. They would smell and it would take me too long to do them. It seemed like it was hard for me to develop new habits. I learned some new habits, though. My current habit is that if I do a couple chores, first and foremost they will be dishes and cat litter. If one thing is going to be done, it will be the thing that makes the house smelly. I don't smell it, but Adam does, and leaving it that way is rude. I do it out of consideration for him, and because it is yucky. I want him to come back to a non-smelly house since smell is something that he is sensitive to.

A habit I had at least from ages fifteen to twenty-two, but less and less as the years went by, was asking too many questions. I remember at least one conversation where I did that with Adam not too long after we moved in with each other. I just kept fixating, wanting to know one more thing, wanting to know one more thing after that, until it was tons of questions. People will see this as something rude, and it is not meant to be, but it is. This is an OCD tic of Asperger's, though, not an intentionally rude mannerism.

My head would loop over and over again on the things I would want to know until I would ask the question. As I have gotten older, I have realized it is okay not to know some things, and it bothers me less. My obsessive nature does not bother me so much.

When I was fifteen, I used to write random stuff in my books all the time as a freakish OCD, and also wrote page numbers for different random things in the book cover. Now, much later, the only time I do any writing is with a pink highlighter, and only for certain books where I will want to come back to that information later, like a book for cats where I wanted to learn certain things.

Another habit I had that I did not realize was weird until it was pointed out to me was how I would think about something older in the conversation and want to come back to it instead of going with the flow of the conversation. Adam is the one who told me that it is okay for conversations to flow another way, and I always remembered that and kept that in mind. On rare occasions, I might speak to someone privately about something they said, but I would never jump back to it anymore. That would be a later-on thing; for now, I let the conversation have the ebb and flow that it is supposed to have.

When I first became a massage therapist it was a lonely job and I was not used to all the quiet time and not talking to people. I have matured and gotten older, and I've stopped having that issue. I am okay with my people time, and I am also okay with my alone time. I have developed a lot of hobbies to do by myself, but I am not obsessed with video games the way that I used to be. There are a lot of things I like to do now.

Photography, videography, reading, writing, watching independent films and documentaries, canoeing, hiking — there are all kinds of things I like to do. So much so, that I can't even do them all and have to make myself do something later. I am glad I am no longer obsessed with video games like I used to be. I am glad I have gotten to see the other things in life. I love singing to music, hearing the notes, singing to the melody; it just feels so nice to me. I love being able to fluctuate the notes to the music and see if I can do it just right.

I have stopped being uncomfortable with people and stopped feeling social anxiety, which I used to have terribly, especially around age fifteen, when all of my symptoms seemed to be at their worst. Now I am not fazed by talking to people, not even by public speaking. Some things we just snap out of as we get older, or as we get enough experience to realize these fears just don't matter, and they get dropped.

It has been nice to see what my life has brought me — all things that would have been nice as a kid but were just not there yet, and they were not meant to be. We know better and do better, every single day, especially with Asperger's. We are a different person every day, with so many lessons and social lessons to learn, just not in the same way as neurotypical or non-Aspies would learn. Common sense to them is different than common sense to us, and we need to learn in our own way.

It is not a bad thing, it just is what it is, and we learn at our own pace. Having behavioral counseling and martial arts would have been nice growing up, but ultimately something that would not happen. I got by the best I could without it. Now, as an adult, if I need help I will pursue it and get a counseling appointment, sort some things out, learn some better solutions for things. If I get angry, depressed, or want to communicate in my relationship better, those are all things that get addressed and I am better for it. Some counselors give amazing feedback. What I have found is one may seem initially expensive, but we will actually save money if their advice is good, because we will not need to come in so much; and it will be good for us if we take their advice as often as possible.

    I am just glad that things have worked out as well as they have for me, and things continue to improve.

Surprise

Adam and I had a trip to Vegas planned for the two of us. I was looking forward to going, and I always have a good time there and enjoy the spas and things. When asked what I wanted for my birthday this year, I replied, "How about a nice spa day?" Adam gave me the works. We went to the MGM grand spa, where I got my nails done, a facial, a massage with knots worked out, and another more relaxing one with a mummy wrap and clay. It was all fancy and good and people were nice, and they were also helpful with knowing what was next on my schedule.

Before the trip, Adam had asked me if I wanted to get married since it had become legal in the United States and things had changed. I said that I would. We had always wanted to but were not able to until then, at least with nothing that would carry over into the state of Arkansas. We'd filled out documents when we got there to make it official, but I was not sure when the wedding would be happening, only that it would happen at some point in the trip.

I was supposed to meet Adam at a certain time and there was only one clock I could find. I daydreamed a little and went back to the clock and realized I was going to be running late. About thirty minutes had just jumped by with a little bit of daydreaming. I raced to get my clothes on as fast as I could and I exited. Adam saw me and we walked over a little ways to meet a man who seemed nice and spoke with me about my thirtieth birthday, and told me how each decade things just got better and better for him.

I felt confused right then. I had the idea that perhaps he had signed me up for an acting class and I did not know what was going on, but this man seemed so nice and seemed "spiritual" somehow, if that makes sense. I walked over to these tables and found that a bunch of people I knew from Arkansas were seated. Our whole Arkansas family was there, and also my sister Erin from Oregon.

I was so confused. I had no idea how they could have gotten there or how it could have been kept a secret from me, but it was. Suddenly we were getting married. I gave my phone to James so that it could be filmed. We held hands and looked into each other's eyes as we repeated what we were asked to repeat. I said my parts with decent volume and with pride. Then I got to give him a nice lovely kiss. I was so happy.

Adam had a group dinner planned for us at Emeril's, and we had the best several-course meal imaginable, which ended with desserts and cakes. We could not eat too much of the desserts, but we had enough anyway, and then we were racing over to watch the Cirque du Soleil show KÀ, which everyone had tickets for, which Adam had planned as well. Adam got to show people how to have a good time. It felt so nice and fancy to walk such a small distance and also see a show.

The trip planned for the two of us became a group trip. It was so exciting and happy I had trouble sleeping that night. I regretted not buying some sleep-aid stuff earlier in the trip a little bit, but it had not seemed necessary then. I slept around it the best I could and had a wonderful rest of the trip, and came back home with Adam, who was now my husband.

www.ingramcontent.com/pod-product-compliance
Lightning Source LLC
Chambersburg PA
CBHW060525080526
44586CB00012B/613